T5-CVS-971

PERSPECTIVES IN LEADER EFFECTIVENESS

LIST OF CONTRIBUTORS

Orlando C. Behling: Ohio State University

Kenneth H. Blanchard: California American University

Paul M. Bons: U.S. Military Academy, West Point

Arthur Elliott Carlisle: University of Massachusetts

Martin M. Chemers: University of Utah, Salt Lake City

Fred E. Fiedler: University of Washington, Seattle

Ronald K. Hambleton: California American University

Paul Hersey: California American University

Robert J. House: University of Toronto

J. G. Hunt: Southern Illinois University of Carbondale

Thomas W. Johnson: Ohio University

James A. Lee: Ohio University

Terence R. Mitchell: University of Washington, Seattle

R. N. Osborn: Southern Illinois University at Carbondale

Chester A. Schriesheim: University of Southern California

Henry P. Sims: Pennsylvania State University

John Stinson: Ohio University

James M. Tolliver: Michigan State University

Victor H. Vroom: Yale University

PERSPECTIVES IN LEADER EFFECTIVENESS

EDITED BY PAUL HERSEY AND JOHN STINSON

The Center for Leadership Studies

Ohio University

Library of Congress Cataloging in Publication Data
Main entry under title:

Perspectives in leader effectiveness.

Includes bibliographical references.
1. Management—Addresses, essays, lectures.
2. Leadership—Addresses, essays, lectures. 3. Organization—Addresses, essays, lectures. I. Stinson, John E. II. Hersey, Paul.
HD38.P4444 658.4 79-14616
ISBN 0-8214-0411-3

ISBN 0-8214-0411-3
Printed in the United States of America by Oberlin Printing Co.
Distributed by Ohio University Press

TABLE OF CONTENTS

INTRODUCTION

During the past several decades researchers have scrutinized leadership effectiveness deeply, reported voluminously, and have developed and tested theories to guide the manager who would emerge or improve. While our knowledge of effective leadership is far from complete, there have been contributions which can be useful to the practicing manager. Too often, however, the dissemination of knowledge to practitioners lags far behind the research and theory development.

This book, which grew out of a concern about the gap between theory and practice, is an attempt to infuse the world of actual management with the body of knowledge produced by the researchers. The volume combines position papers on the current state of leadership knowledge, examinations of leadership theories, and anecdotal examples of effective leadership.

The volume is divided into four parts. Part I, "Some Early Contributions," puts leadership in perspective and examines the development of leadership thought. Part II, "Power and Decision Making," focuses on the role of power in a leader's decision making. In Part III—"Leader, Follower, and Task"—contemporary situational theories of leadership are examined. Part IV, "Examples of Effective Leadership," offers the reader a chance to follow the application of leadership theories. The major thrust of each chapter is highlighted below.

The Ohio State Leadership Studies early explored leader behavior and the importance of its impact on organizational effectiveness. In Chapter I Schriesheim, Tolliver, and Behling, concentrating on the Ohio State Studies, trace the development of leadership thought and view leadership from the perspective of total managerial activities.

Fred Fiedler was an early proponent of the contingency or situational approach in contrast with the one "best" leadership style. In Chapter II he, Chemers, and Bons review Fiedler's "Contingency Theory of Leadership Effectiveness" and discuss the latest extension of the theory "Leader Match."

A discussion of leadership is incomplete without an examination of the role of power and influence. James Lee, in Chapter III, explores the impact that social changes have had on the distribution of power in organizations. He presents a leader-power system model to illustrate the limitations on the power available to the organizational leader of today. Power is also a central concept in Hunt and Osborne's "Multiple-Influence Approach to Leadership." In Chapter IV, after defining discretionary and non-discretionary leadership, Hunt and Osborne examine the factors which limit discretion and detail how these limitations affect choice of behavior style.

Part of the leader's role is decision making, and the first problem is to determine who should make decisions. Vroom, in Chapter V, presents a model of decision-making styles and the parameters of the environment which influence the leader's choice of decision-making style.

In Chapter VI House and Mitchell view the helping role the leader plays in reference to the environment. They discuss the "Path-Goal Theory of Leadership," which proposes that the effectiveness of a leader is influenced by the follower's environment, particularly by the nature of the follower's job.

Hersey and Blanchard offer, in Chapter VII, their "Situational Leadership Theory" and explore its application to the relationship between leader and follower in formal and informal systems of Management by Objectives. They emphasize the importance of contracting for the role of the leader as well as for the objectives of the follower.

In Chapter VIII Stinson and Johnson further explore the relationship between leader, follower, and environment and present a situational model which incorporates leader strategies, the personality of the follower, and the nature of the follower's job.

Sims, in Chapter IX, narrates the problems of a manager who searches for a method to improve the performance of an employee. Sims illustrates the importance of reinforcing positive behaviors and of avoiding the reinforcement of negative behaviors.

In Chapter X Carlisle introduces the manager who has made delegating a fine art. He explores the manager's approach to leadership and discusses situations which influence the manager's effectiveness.

Many people have provided assistance in the preparation of this book. While it is not possible to recognize all by name, we would like to thank particularly our contributors, who took time from their crowded schedules to write the chapters which make up the book.

Part 1

SOME EARLY CONTRIBUTIONS

Chapter 1

LEADERSHIP: SOME ORGANIZATIONAL AND MANAGERIAL IMPLICATIONS

Chester A. Schriesheim

James M. Tolliver

Orlando C. Behling

To pick up almost any book dealing with management is to find some discussion of "leadership." To go through any company library is to find a host of volumes entitled "increasing leadership effectiveness," "successful leadership," or "how to lead." A look at the typical management development programs, conducted both within work organizations and universities, reveals that a substantial number of these are concerned with some aspect of "leadership." In sum, the intensity and duration of writings on leadership and the vast sums spent annually on leadership training both indicate that both academicians and practicing managers consider good leadership important to organizational success.

What is meant by "leadership," let alone good leadership? Although many definitions have been proposed, most of these treat leadership in terms of interpersonal interactions among a "leader" and one or more "subordinates," with the purpose being to increase organizational effectiveness.[1] Other aspects of the managerial job, such as monitoring and controlling resources, are usually ignored in these conceptualizations. This oversight occurs despite the fact that these other types of managerial tasks may, in fact, have stronger impacts on organizational effectiveness than those interpersonal tasks usually labeled as "leadership."[2] However, despite this shortcoming in current approaches to leadership, the examination of leadership as dealing with interpersonal interactions still seems worthwhile. This is true because managers may really have more control over how they and their subordinates *behave* than those nonhuman aspects of their jobs such as the amount and types of resources they are given.

Approaches to Leadership: A Brief Review

Over three thousand studies have been conducted during the past 70 years in the area of leadership, and dozens of theories and models have been proposed.[3] However, despite this overwhelming volume of theoretical and research activity, few practical guides still exist for the manager. Thus, before attempting to provide some useful guidelines, we shall briefly review some of the major historical approaches to leadership and point out their practical weaknesses and limitations.

The study of leadership has moved through three distinct periods or phases: the *trait phase*, the *behavioral phase*, and the *situational phase*. All three of these have some unique characteristics, and these are noted on the following pages. Figure 1 shows these phases in the development of leadership thought in diagrammatic form.

The trait phase. Early approaches to leadership, from before the birth of Christ to the late 1940's, emphasized the examination of leader characteristics (such as age and degree of gregariousness) in an attempt to

Figure 1
The Development of Leadership Thought

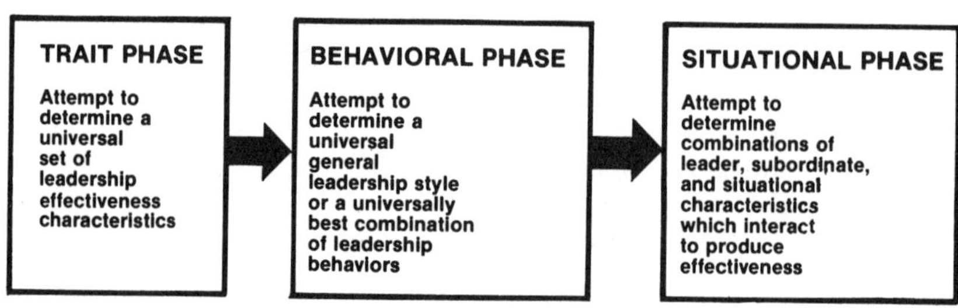

identify a set of *universal* characteristics which allow leaders to be effective in *all* situations. Although a few traits emerged as seemingly important in some studies, the research results on these were not consistent, and the research on the remainder was generally negative. As a result of this accumulation of negative findings and of reviews of this evidence such as that conducted by Stogdill, the tide of opinion about the importance of traits began to change in the late 1940's, and leadership researchers began to move away from "trait research," most never to return to it again.[4] Contemporary opinion currently holds the trait approach in considerable disrepute and deems as essentially impossible the likelihood of uncovering a set of *universal* leadership effectiveness traits.

The behavioral phase. With the fall of the trait approach researchers in leadership considered a number of alternative concepts, eventually settling on the examination of relationships among leader behaviors and subordinate satisfaction and performance.[5] During the height of the behavioral phase, dating roughly from the late 1940's to the early 1960's, several large research programs were conducted, including The Ohio State University Leadership studies, a program of research which has received considerable publicity over the years.

The Ohio State Leadership studies started shortly after World War II and, in the beginning, concentrated on leadership in military organizations. In one of these studies, a lengthy questionnaire was administered to B-52 bomber crews, and their answers were subjected to statistical analysis which can identify the common dimensions underlying a large set of answers.[6] From this analysis two dimensions were uncovered which seemed most important in summarizing the nature of the crews' perceptions about their airplane commanders' behavior towards them:

1. *Consideration* was the strongest of the two factors, and it involved leader behaviors which were "indicative of friendship, mutual trust, respect, and warmth."[7]
2. *Initiation of Structure*, a concept involving leader behaviors "which indicate that the (leader) . . . organizes and defines the relationship between himself and the members of the crew."[8]

In subsequent studies, in which modified versions of the original questionnaire were used, consideration and structure were found to be prime dimensions of leader behavior in a variety of different situations, ranging from flying combat missions over Korea to assembly line work.[9] In addition, a large number of studies were undertaken, both at Ohio State and elsewhere, to compare the effects of these leader behaviors on subordinate performance and satisfaction. A high consideration-high structure leadership style was often found to lead to high performance and satisfaction. However, in a number of studies dysfunctional consequences (such as high turnover and absenteeism), accompanied these positive outcomes, and in other cases other combinations of consideration and structure (i.e., low consideration-high structure) were found to be more effective.[10]

Similar behaviors were identified and similar results obtained in other studies, such as those conducted at the University of Michigan.[11] So, while the display of highly considerate-highly structuring behavior was found to result sometimes in positive organizational outcomes, *this was not true in all cases or even most.*[12] The research clearly indicated that no single leadership style was universally effective, for the relationships among supervisory behavior, organizational performance, and employee satisfaction changed from situation to situation. By the early 1960's this fact had become apparent, and the orientation of leadership researchers began to change towards a situational approach.

The situational phase. Current research in leadership is now almost entirely directed toward the situational. The situational approach examines the interrelationships among leader and subordinate behaviors or characteristics and the situation (s) in which they find themselves. This can clearly be seen in the other papers which comprise this volume, for example in the work of Fiedler, who outlines how such factors interact to produce leadership effectiveness. In summary, Fiedler's theory is that relationship-motivated leaders display task-orientated behaviors (such as structure) in situations which are favorable to their exertion of influence over their work group, and display relationship-oriented behaviors (such as consideration) in situations which are either moderately favorable or unfavorable. Task-motivated leaders, on the other hand, display relationship-oriented behaviors in favorable situations and task-oriented behaviors in both moderately favorable and unfavorable situations. Fiedler's model specifies that relationship-motivated leaders will be more effective than task-motivated leaders in situations which are moderately favorable for leader exertion of influence, but that the opposite will hold true in more favorable and less favorable situations.

House and Mitchell, Vroom, and the other authors in this volume propose similar types of interactions between the leader, the led, and the situation. We will not review these other models, but the reader should be able to grasp the general orientation of the situational approach to leadership from our discussion of Fiedler's model.

Although most of these newer situational models have not been fully tested, the existent research generally supports the notion that a situational view of leadership is necessary to portray accurately the complexities involved in leadership processes.

Implications

The reader might well ask at this point "What does all this discussion of leadership theory and research have to do with the *practice* of management?" Several answers to this question exist, both for organizations attempting to increase the effectiveness of leaders within the managerial and supervisory ranks and for individual managers concerned with self-development. Although the two implications to be drawn are intertwined, we attempt to treat them separately in the following sections.

Organizational Implications

First, *selection* does not seem to be the primary answer as far as organizational efforts to increase the pool of effective leaders are concerned. The results of the numerous-trait studies summarized by Stogdill and others clearly indicate that the search for universal personality characteristics of effective leaders is almost certainly doomed to failure.[13] Even this statement deserves some qualification, however. It should be recognized that this assertion concerns *leadership* effectiveness, which is only one aspect of *managerial* effectiveness. A manager may contribute to organizational effectiveness in many different ways other than by being an effective leader. The selection of effective managers, as distinguished from effective leaders, may be more important than is generally realized. Further, present disappointment with attempts at leader selection results from research which has sought to identify universal characteristics that typify effective leaders in all situations. Summaries such as Stogdill's demonstrate that leadership effectiveness is highly dependent upon the relationship between leader characteristics and the demands of particular situations, and thus universal approaches will not work.[14] However, exploration of leader traits in the context of *particular situations* may reveal that careful selection of likely managers has some potential. Unfortunately, given the number of situational factors which appear to influence leadership effectiveness, it seems unlikely that any managerial selection procedure designed to maximize leadership effectiveness will resemble typical actuarial (statistical) selection procedures.[15] It appears almost impossible for a firm to gather enough individuals in jobs identical along crucial dimensions to provide the basis for a conventional actuarial validation study. This does not preclude, however, the possibility of the use of clinical (judgmental) techniques for selection of leaders.

A further limitation on selection procedures as ways of increasing the pool of effective managers within organizations is the dynamic nature of managerial jobs and of the careers of managers. If, as research seems to indicate, leadership success is situation-specific, then the continual and inevitable shifts in the nature of a manager's assignment and his movement from one assignment to another may make the initial selection invalid.

Another implication is that existing forms of managerial leadership training, based on the body of evidence outlined here, appear to be inappropriate. Two reasons exist for this. First, the vast majority of training programs are based upon the assumption that a "one best way to manage" (a best leadership style) exists, and this is usually seen as either one which places a high degree of emphasis on an employee-centered (considerate) approach or which combines a concern for employees with a concern for high output (initiating structure). For example, the "Managerial Grid" and its associated "Grid Organizational Development Program" are currently quite popular approaches to management and organizational development.[16] Both are based upon the premise that a managerial style which shows high concern for people and high concern for production "is acknowledged universally . . . as the soundest way to achieve excellence," and both attempt to develop this style of behavior on the part of all managers.[17] Likert's "System-Four" approach to managerial and organizational development, although different from the Grid approach, also assumes that a "one best way to manage" exists (employee-centered leadership).[18] Clearly, these ideas are in conflict with both the research summarized earlier and with contemporary "scholarly" opinion. The chapters by Fiedler, House and Mitchell and by the other authors in this volume clearly indicate that there is no single style which is appropriate to all situations. House and Mitchell also suggest that the application of highly employee-centered or combined styles may actually lead to long-run *negative* impacts on both job performance and satisfaction (in situations which provide adequate direct sources of job satisfaction and task clarity).

The second limitation of leadership training is that it seems to be basically ineffective in changing the behaviors of the individual participants. Leadership training aimed not directly at leadership behavior itself but rather at providing diagnostic skills for the identification of the situation and the behaviors appropriate to it appears to offer considerable potential for the improvement of leadership effectiveness. Obviously, however, considerable additional research is required to identify the dimensions of situations crucial to leadership performance and the styles effective under various circumstances before such training can be offered with any degree of confidence.

Fiedler's suggestion that organizations "engineer the job to fit the manager" also offers some potential, but, in our opinion, it suffers from some of the same problems encountered by attempts to train leaders.[19] The basic idea of modifying the crucial characteristics of the situation to make it appropriate to the manager's personal leadership style is appealing, if somewhat utopian. The fact that we have not as yet clearly identified the crucial dimensions of situations which affect leadership performance appears to be a limitation on the application of this approach. Also, while the overall approach may well offer considerable theoretical advantage when leadership is treated in isolation, it ignores the possible dysfunctional consequences on other aspects of the organization's operations. Maximizing leadership effectiveness *alone* cannot be the only consideration of administrators as they make decisions about job assignments and the like. They must consider a variety of other aspects of the organization's operations which may conflict with their attempts to maximize the effectiveness of existing leadership talent. Within these limitations, however, this idea does offer some potential for improving organizational performance through increases in leadership effectiveness.

One final comment on organizational implications of leadership theory and research seems appropriate before a discussion of its implications for individual managers. Although generally discredited in the academic world, it is not at all unusual for work organizations to use traits and trait descriptions in evaluations of managerial performance. A quick glance at the typical performance rating form reveals the presence of terms such as "personality" and "attitude" as factors for the evaluation of managers. Clearly, these terms represent a modern-day version of the traits investigated 30 years ago, and they may or may not be related to actual job performance (depending upon the specifics of the situation involved). Some explicit rationale and, hopefully, evidence that such traits do in fact affect managerial performance is needed before they are included in performance evaluations; (just "feeling" that they are "important" is *not* sufficient justification).

Individual Implications

The implications of our discussion of leadership theory and research for individual managers are fewer in number and, as we indicated, are intertwined with those for total organizations. The fact that leadership effectiveness is not dependent upon a single set of personal characteristics with which an individual is born or which he acquires at an early age should provide a sense of relief to many managers and potential managers. This conclusion indicates that success in leadership is not limited to a small elite but rather can be attained by almost any individual, assuming that the situation is proper or that the manager can adjust to it. The process leading to effective leadership, in other words, is not so much one of changing the characteristics of the individual as it is one of either assuring that he is placed in a situation appropriate to his particular pattern of behavior or teaching him how to modify his behavior to fit the situation.

Thus the individual manager can improve his managerial and leadership effectiveness primarily through the development of skills in analyzing the nature of organizational situations, both task and interpersonal demands, so that he can determine the appropriateness of his particular managerial style for the particular situation. Although providing guidelines concerning how a manager might generally act is difficult, some recent research aids in the development of a number of tentative prescriptions.[20]

Generally speaking, it appears that a high consideration-high structure style often works best. However, this approach cannot be applied in *all* instances because, as we have already noted, sometimes dysfunctional consequences result from the display of highly considerate and highly structuring behaviors. For example, higher management sometimes gives highly considerate managers poor performance ratings, while in other instances high structure has been related to employee dissatisfaction, grievances, and turnover. Thus, it appears that it is sometimes necessary for the manager to choose between high consideration and high structure, and it is here that diagnostic ability becomes important.

In these instances, as a general rule, it seems safe to say that while high consideration alone is no guarantee of subordinate performance, its positive effects on frustration-instigated types of behavior are probably enough to warrant its recommendation as a general style. However, a number of situations exist where structure should probably be emphasized, although it may or may not mean a decrease in subordinate perceptions of consideration. Although the following do not constitute an exhaustive listing of these exceptions, they do comprise those which are known and appear important at the present time. The individual manager has to add such additional ones as he can identify in his situation.

Emergencies or high-pressure situation. Where physical danger is involved in the work, when time is limited, or when little tolerance exists for errors, emphasis on initiating structure is probably desirable. Research demonstrates that in such instances subordinates often expect and prefer the leader to exhibit a high structure style.

Situations where there is one source of information. In instances where the leader is the only person knowledgeable about the task, subordinates often expect him to make specific job assignments, set deadlines, and engage in structuring behaviors in general. At the same time, however, there is often little reason why the leader cannot be considerate as well.

Untrained or inexperienced subordinates. Where the subordinate is relatively unknowledgeable because of lack of training or experience, leader provision of structure may be viewed as supportive and helpful. However, where subordinates are experienced or knowledgeable, structuring behavior may be seen as threatening.

Subordinate preferences. There is limited evidence that some subordinates prefer high structure and expect it, while others expect low consideration and are suspicious of leaders who display high consideration. Other preference patterns undoubtedly exist, and the manager should attempt to tailor his behavior towards each individual subordinate.

Preferences of higher management. Research indicates that in some instances higher management has definite preferences for different leadership styles. For example, in some cases higher management has preferred and expected high structure and low consideration and has rewarded managers for displaying this behavioral style. Thus, it would appear that the manager should be sensitive to the desires of his superiors in addition to those of his subordinates. Unfortunately, it is not possible to specify how these expectations may be reconciled if they diverge.

Leader ability to adjust. A final consideration is the ability of the leader to adjust his behavior to fit the situation. Some managers will be able to do this. For others, attempts to modify their behavior may appear to subordinates to be false and manipulative. In these instances, the manager would probably be better off retaining the style with which he is most comfortable.

Limitations and Conclusions

The situational approach we have been advocating in this chapter avoids the major shortcoming of both the trait and behavioral approaches to leadership. However, we should point out that we have assumed, perhaps implicitly, that hierarchical leadership is always important and that recently this assumption has come under increasing questioning. Kerr, for example, points out that many factors may limit the ability of a hierarchical superior to act as a "leader" for subordinates.[21] Factors such as technology (i.e., the assembly line), training, clear job descriptions, and the like may provide subordinates with enough guidance so that supervisor structure (or similar behaviors) may be unnecessary to help ensure task performance. Likewise, jobs which are intrinsically satisfying may negate the need for supervisor consideration, since consideration is not needed to offset job dullness or routinization.

Another problem with our approach, and with leadership as a major emphasis in general, is that (as we briefly suggested in our introduction to this chapter) effective leadership may account for only 10-15 percent of the variability in unit performance.[22] While 10-15 percent is certainly not a trivial amount, it is clear that much of what affects performance in organizations is not being accounted for by "leadership." Thus, while studying and emphasizing leadership certainly has merit, it could equally well be argued that there is much to be gained by widening our sights to treat leadership effectiveness as but one of the components of *managerial effectiveness*. As we have emphasized in an earlier publication:

> It is necessary to note that leadership is only one way in which the manager contributes to organizational effectiveness. The manager also performs duties which are *externally oriented* so far as his unit is concerned. For example, he may spend part of his time coordinating the work of his unit with other units. Similarly, not all of the manager's *internally oriented* activities can be labeled leadership acts. Some of them concern the physical and organizational conditions under which the work unit operates. For example, the manager spends part of his time obtaining resources (materials, equipment, manpower, and so on) necessary for unit operations. This is an essentially internally oriented activity but hardly constitutes leadership. Clearly, the manager must perform a mix of internal and external activities if his unit is to perform well. Leadership is only one of the internal activities performed by managers.[23]

Thus, we must caution the practicing manager *not* to overemphasize the importance of leadership activities, especially if this causes other important managerial functions to be neglected.

In summary, what we have suggested in this chapter is that for managers to be effective as leaders, they must attempt to be flexible and to tailor their behaviors to account for differences in subordinates and situations. We have also tried to put leadership in perspective. Both organizations and individual managers must be wary of attempting to maximize leadership effectiveness if this attempt entails a reduction in effectiveness in other aspects of the managerial job. Clearly, leadership is important, but it cannot be treated in isolation—the importance of leadership is undoubtedly situational, and the practicing manager must take this into account.

NOTES

1. C. A. Gibb, "Leadership," In G. Lindzey & E. Aronson (Eds.), *The Handbook of Social Psychology*, Vol. 4 (Reading, Mass: Addison-Wesley, 1969).

2. J. P. Campbell, M. D. Dunnette, E. E. Lawler, & K. E. Weick, *Managerial Behavior, Performance, and Effectiveness*. (New York: McGraw-Hill, 1970).

3. R. M. Stogdill, *Handbook of Leadership*. (New York: The Free Press, 1974).

4. R. M. Stogdill, "Personal Factors Associated with Leadership: A Survey of the Literature." *The Journal of Psychology*, 1948, 25, pp. 35-72.

5. T. O. Jacobs, *Leadership and Exchange in Formal Organizations.* (Alexandria, Va.: Human Resources Research Organization, 1970).

6. A. W. Halpin & B. J. Winer, "A Factorial Study of the Leader Behavior Descriptions." In R. M. Stogdill & A. E. Coons (Eds.), *Leader Behavior: Its Description and Measurement.* (Columbus: Ohio State University, Bureau of Business Research, 1957.)

7. *Ibid.*, p. 42.

8. *Ibid.*

9. R. M. Stogdill & A. E. Coons, *Leader Behavior: Its Description and Measurement.* Columbus: The Ohio State University, Bureau of Business Research, 1957.

10. S. Kerr, C. Schriesheim, C. J. Murphy, & R. M. Stogdill, "Toward a Contingency Theory of Leadership Based upon the Consideration and Initiating Structure Literature." *Organizational Behavior and Human Performance*, 1974, 12, pp. 62-82.

11. D. Katz, N. Maccoby & N. Morse, *Productivity, Supervision and Morale in an Office Situation.* (Ann Arbor, Mi: University of Michigan, Survey Research Center, 1951).

12. Kerr et al., *op. cit.*, 1974.

13. Stogdill, *op. cit.*

14. *Ibid.*

15. Kerr et al., *op. cit.* 1974.

16. R. R. Blake & J. S. Mouton, *The Managerial Grid.* (Houston, Texas: Gulf, 1964) and R. R. Blake & J. S. Mouton, *Building a Dynamic Corporation Through Grid Organization Development.* (Reading, Mass: Addison-Wesley, 1969).

17. Blake & Mouton, 1969, *op. cit.*, p. 63.

18. R. Likert, *New Patterns of Management.* (New York: McGraw-Hill, 1961) and R. Likert, *The Human Organization: Its Management and Value.* (New York: McGraw-Hill, 1967).

19. F. E. Fiedler, "Engineer the Job to Fit the Manager," *Harvard Business Review*, 1965, 43, pp. 115-122.

20. Kerr et al., *op. cit.*, 1974.

21. *Ibid.*

22. O. Behling & C. Schriesheim, *Organizational Behavior: Theory, Research and Application.* (Boston: Allyn and Bacon, 1976).

23. *Ibid.*

Chapter 2

IMPLICATIONS OF THE CONTINGENCY MODEL FOR IMPROVING ORGANIZATIONAL EFFECTIVENESS

Fred E. Fiedler
Martin M. Chemers
Paul M. Bons

This chapter briefly describes a theory of leadership, the *Contingency Model*, its implications for management practice, and the development of a training program for more effective leadership. This theory states that the performance of either a group or an organization depends on (or is contingent upon) the degree to which the leader's personality matches the requirements of the leadership situation. According to this theory, certain types of individuals are primarily motivated to seek close interpersonal relations while others are primarily motivated by the esteem which comes from accomplishing a task. Task-motivated individuals perform best in situations which provide a high degree of control and influence and in situations in which their control and influence are very low. Relationship-motivated people perform best in situations in which their control and influence are moderate. In other words, both the task-motivated and the relationship-motivated leaders can be highly effective if they are in situations which match their particular personalities.

The leader's motivation, that is, whether the leader is task- or relationship-motivated, is measured by means of a simple adjective checklist. The individual is asked to think of everyone with whom he or she has ever worked and then to describe the one person who was most difficult to work with, the "least preferred coworker." This scale contains such items as "pleasant-unpleasant, friendly-unfriendly, tense-relaxed," etc., and the LPC (least preferred coworker) score indicates how positive or negative the leader perceives this least preferred coworker. The description of the least preferred coworker then identifies the leader as being either a relationship-motivated (high LPC) or a task-motivated (low LPC) person.

Note that the LPC score denotes how the leader perceives his or her least preferred coworker. However, this description in fact indicates the leader's own basic goals in a worker situation. An individual who describes the least preferred coworker in a negative, rejecting manner (a low LPC) in effect tells us that the completion of the task is of such overriding importance that it completely determines the way in which he will regard the person with whom he cannot work: "If I cannot work with you, if you frustrate my need to accomplish the task, then you can't be any good in other respects. You are . . . unpleasant, unfriendly, cold, rejecting, if not totally worthless."

The individual who sees his or her least preferred coworker in a more positive manner (high LPC) tells us, in effect, that getting the task accomplished is not really everything in life: "Even if I can't work with you, you may still be relatively pleasant, friendly, interesting, etc., and I might even like to be with you socially."

The other major element in the theory is the *degree to which the situation provides the leader with control and influence*. A high degree of control and influence means that the leader has considerable certainty that his decisions and actions will have predictable outcomes, that they will achieve the ends he desires—namely, that they will satisfy the leader's needs either for a close relationship or for the accomplishment of the task. Incidentally, when we have certainty about the future, we do not feel anxious and under stress, and people act quite differently when they are relaxed and secure from when they are anxious and tense. Some become more efficient while others fall apart when stress is high; some become bored and disinterested in what they are doing when stress is low, and still others can concentrate more when they are in complete control of the situation and can predict exactly what's going to happen.

Determination of Situational Control

Situational control or favorableness, as it was originally called, has most frequently been measured by means of three subscales. The first of these indicates the degree to which leader-member relations are good; that is, the degree to which the leader enjoys the support and loyalty of group members. This dimension is assessed either by means of sociometric preference ratings completed by group members about the leader, by a set of self-rated descriptive items, or by a group-atmosphere scale which the leader fills out.

The *leader-member relations* dimension is the most important of the three subscales since a leader who enjoys the support and loyalty of group members can depend and rely on them. He can be certain that the group members will do their best to comply with his wishes and directions. The leader who cannot count on his group is, of course, in a very precarious position. He will need to be considerably more circumspect in his dealings with subordinates and continuously on guard to assure that his directions or policies are not subverted. Illustrative items from a recent scale are:

The people I supervise have trouble getting along with each other.
Strongly agree :___:___:___:___:___: Strongly disagree
1 2 3 4 5

My subordinates are reliable and trustworthy.
Strongly agree :___:___:___:___:___: Strongly disagree
1 2 3 4 5

There seems to be a friendly atmosphere among the people I supervise.
Strongly agree :___:___:___:___:___: Strongly disagree
1 2 3 4 5

The second most important dimension of the leadership situation is *task structure*. We generally do not think of the task as providing leaders with control and influence. However, leaders who have a blueprint or detailed operating instructions are assured of the support of their organization in directing the job and can feel assured that they are proceeding in the right direction. They very rarely get any arguments from subordinates about the course the group should take. In contrast, when the task is unstructured, as is the case with typical committee assignments or research and development work, the control which leaders can exercise over the task and the group is considerably diluted. In fact, a committee chairperson would find it extremely difficult to dictate the course of the work or to predict the acceptability of the outcome. Such a prediction is easily made when the leader has step-by-step instructions which guarantee an acceptably completed task if they are faithfully followed.

The degree of task structure has been measured in a number of ways, generally by four subcategories suggested by Shaw. These are (1) the degree to which the goal of this task is clear, (2) the degree to which the final task product can be evaluated and/or verified, (3) the number of different task solutions or products which might be acceptable, and (4) the number of different ways there are for undertaking the task. Measuring scales for each of these four subscales have been developed by Hunt and have been described in previous publications.[1] Abbreviated scales also have been extensively used and generally serve the purpose quite well. By and large, line management, production supervisors, and military troop commanders have relatively structured tasks. Leaders of research and development groups, committees, boards, or organizations which require creative effort tend to have unstructured tasks. Examples from a recent scale are:

Is there a blueprint, picture, model, or detailed description available of the finished product or service?

2	1	0
Usually True	Sometimes True	Seldom True

Is the evaluation of this task generally made on some quantitative basis?

2	1	0
Usually True	Sometimes True	Seldom True

Are there some ways which are clearly recognized as better than others for performing this task?

2	1	0
Usually True	Sometimes True	Seldom True

Is it obvious when the task is finished and the correct solution has been found?

2	1	0
Usually True	Sometimes True	Seldom True

The third dimension which defines situational control is *position power, i.e.*, the degree to which leaders are able to reward and punish, to recommend sanctions, or otherwise to enforce compliance by subordinates. A scale of position power would include such questions as, "Can the leader directly or by recommendation administer rewards and punishments to subordinates?", "Can the leader directly or by recommendation affect promotion, demotion, hiring, or firing of subordinates?", "Is it the leader's job to evaluate the performance of subordinates?", etc. Here, again, a scale is available which provides norms for scoring.[2]

The leader's overall situational control is usually designated on an eight-point dimension. This index is obtained by dividing the groups into those falling above and below the cutting score on the leader-member relations scale, then on the task-structure scale, and finally on the position power scale (See Figure 1). This means that the leader-member relations scale is counted four times as much as position power, and task structure is counted twice as much as position power. Several empirical studies have shown that this weighting scheme is quite accurate.

Figure 1
SITUATIONAL CONTROL

LEADER-MEMBER RELATIONS	Good				Poor			
TASK STRUCTURE	Structured		Unstructured		Structured		Unstructured	
POSITION POWER	Strong	Weak	Strong	Weak	Strong	Weak	Strong	Weak
CELL	1	2	3	4	5	6	7	8

We said earlier that the Contingency Model shows that task-motivated leaders perform best in situations in which their control is high or else very low, and that relationship-motivated leaders perform better in situations in which they enjoy moderate control. A substantial number of studies have supported this statement. Figure 2 presents a schematic representation on which the degree of situational control is shown on the horizontal axis, with high control on the left, and low control on the right side of the graph. The vertical axis indicates leadership performance or organizational effectiveness with the more effective performance toward the top of the line.

The performance of the relationship-motivated (high LPC) leader is indicated by the solid line in the graph while the performance of the task-motivated leader (low LPC) is shown by the broken line. As can be seen, the task-motivated leaders tend to perform best in the high and the low control situations, and the relationship-motivated leaders generally perform best in the moderate control situation. We can also see from this graph that both

Figure 2
SCHEMATIC REPRESENTATION OF THE CONTINGENCY MODEL

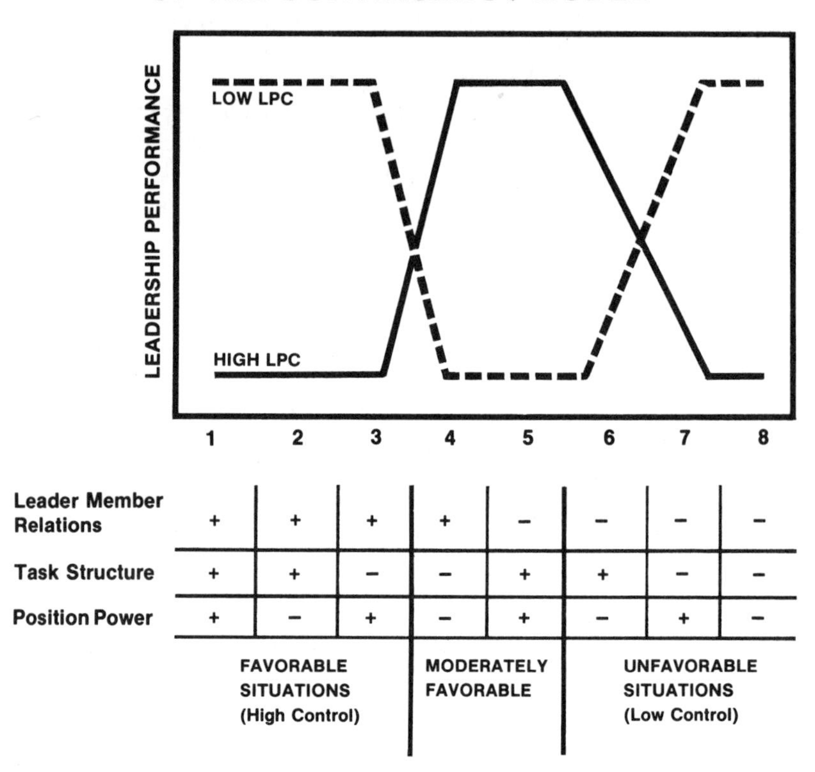

types of leaders will be effective under some conditions but not others. Most importantly, this graph shows that a shift in the situational control will affect the performance of the leader. Thus, if a task-motivated leader finds himself in a moderate-control situation, his performance is likely to go up if he gains greater control over his situation, or even if his control decreases. Likewise, if a relationship-motivated leader finds himself in a high- or a low-control situation and performs poorly, a shift toward the moderate control situation will tend to increase his performance.

A substantial number of studies tested this theory. Not all of these, obviously, have provided unequivocal support. Yet, in 45 sets of groups reviewed by Fiedler in 1971, the results of not fewer than 36 (80%) were in the predicted direction. The most convincing evidence comes from a series of well controlled studies in which the relevant variables of the leader's LPC score and situational control dimensions were carefully measured or strongly manipulated.

One such study was conducted by Chemers and Skrzypek at the U.S. Military Academy at West Point. LPC scores as well as sociometric preference measures were obtained about three weeks before the experiment. Each of 32 groups performed one structured and one unstructured task, with half the groups under a leader with strong position power and one with weak position power. The results of this study almost exactly matched the predictions of the Contingency Model.

Similarly, studies by Hardy and by Hardy, Sack, and Harpine supported the theory. Here again, LPC scores as well as preference scores were obtained prior to the experiment, and the groups were then assembled on the basis of these predetermined LPC and leader-member relations scores. The subjects in these studies were high school students, college seniors, and elementary school children, respectively. In each of the studies, the predictions of the Contingency Model were supported in the various situations. Finally, a field study, conducted by Fiedler, O'Brien, and Ilgen dealt with small public health volunteer teams which worked in Central America. This study was based on LPC scores obtained about three to six weeks prior to the assembly of teams (although team assembly here was not made on the basis of LPC scores). All teams had weak leader position power; some teams worked under stressful conditions (low task structure), others under relatively less stressful conditions, thus testing approximately octants 2, 4, 4, and 8 (See Figure 2). In all of these cells, the performance outcomes were in the predicted direction and significant in cells 6 and 8.

Selection

Let us now consider some of the major implications of the theory for selection and placement of organizational leaders. We generally think of the selection process as requiring that we place round pegs into round holes and square pegs into square holes. This is a neat and easily understood notion except that it completely ignores the fact that the shapes of the pegs and holes change, that is, that the leadership situation is dynamic rather than static and that the individual who will occupy the leadership position will also change.

Typically, change in the individual takes place as he or she gains in experience and knowledge on the job, or as the job itself changes over time. We can predict with considerable confidence that the leader's control and influence will increase as these changes occur. In effect, the task itself will become more structured, and usually the interpersonal relations between leader and group members will become closer. Thus, referring to Figure 2, we will expect that the individual's situational control will shift toward the left of the horizontal axis. According to the theory, a task-motivated leader, who starts out in a low-control situation in which performance is good, will, in time, move into a moderate-control situation and perform relatively less well. At the same time, the relationship-motivated leader, who performs poorly in the low-control situation, should improve in performance as he gains in experience and moves into the moderate control zone.

In the case of a leadership job which starts out in the moderate-control zone, we would expect exactly the reverse. That is, the relationship-motivated leader should perform well in the beginning and gradually become less effective as his or her experience makes the job fall into the high control zone; the task-motivated leader, who performs poorly in the moderate zone, will improve as his or her increasing job experience provides relatively high situational control.

Let us take, for example, a production supervisor newly promoted into a department with which he is unfamiliar. As the supervisor begins the new job, some of the tasks will be strange, and the supervisor will be uncertain about the exact duties and responsibilities of the job. The supervisor will also not be sure of the actual power which the new position provides or how far to go in disciplining an old employee. How should a problem with a supervisor of another shop be handled? Should a complaint be filed or should the problem be handled personally? Can the supervisor discuss with the boss disagreements between employees or should everything look as if it were in good shape?

After several months or years on the job, the supervisor will know the answers to all these questions, which will, undoubtedly, have occurred many times before. The supervisor will have learned how to deal with the boss, with subordinates, and with others in the plant. The leadership situation will have become markedly higher in the amount of control it provides. When the supervisor first started, the leadership situation probably fell into the moderate-control zone. Now, after several years, it probably falls into the high-control zone. Depending on whether the supervisor was task or relationship-motivated, performance will have increased or decreased.

As we know only too well, there are some people who become careless, bored, stale, and disinterested when the job no longer presents a challenge, while others become intrigued with the prospect of making a job more efficient and fine-tuning the system. The effect will be a decrease in the performance of the former and an increase in the performance of the latter.

That these changes do, in fact, occur can be seen from a number of studies, two of which are described here. The first one presents data from a newly formed infantry division. The squad leaders, who supervise 8-11 enlisted men, came into a situation in which they had the problem of making an effective unit of their squad. The recruits knew very little about the army, the officers had their own problems, and the organization—as is true of any organization during the formative stages—was in a condition of flux. Each of the leaders was rated by two or more superiors during the first month of the period. The same leaders were rated again by the same superiors five months later, when the organization had settled down and the sergeants and their subordinates had additional experience in working with one another. As we can see from Figure 3, there was a complete reversal in performance. While the relationship-motivated squad leaders were generally rated more highly in the beginning of the training cycle (a moderate-control situation), the task-motivated squad leaders were rated as performing better toward the end of the training cycle (a high-control situation).

Figure 3

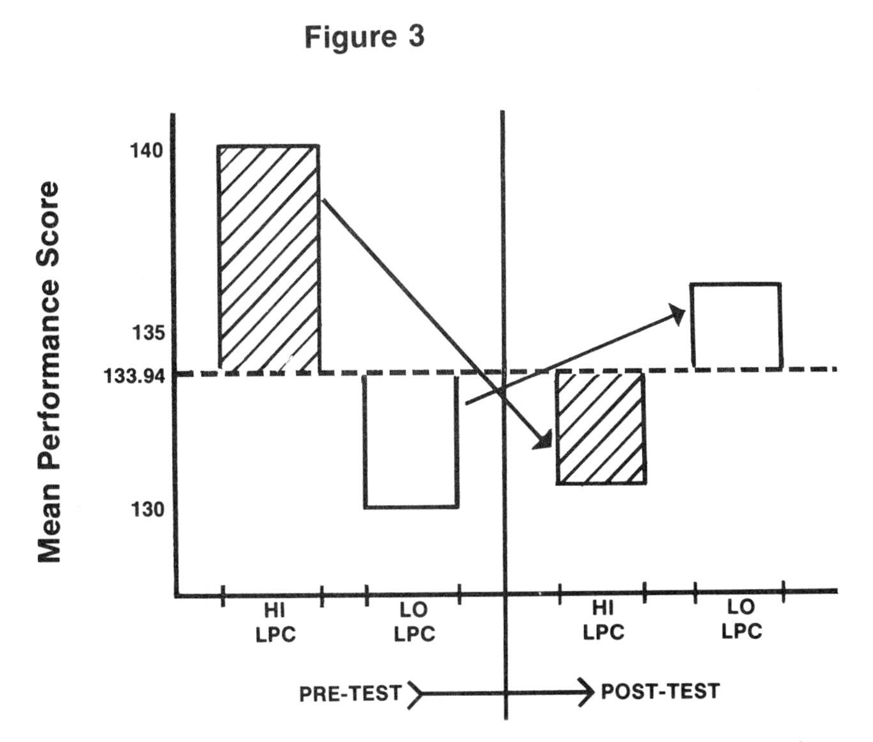

Change in the performance of high and low LPC leaders as a function of increased experience and more structured task assignment over five months.

A similar finding comes from the general managers of a consumer cooperative federation. The criterion of performance was the operating efficiency as a ratio to total sales. This group of managers was divided into those with high or low experience and into those with high or low LPC scores. Here again the task-motivated (low LPC) managers performed relatively poorly if they had little experience but relatively well if their experience was high. This again suggests that task-motivated managers improve as their situation changes from moderate to high control. Similar findings have been reported for school administrators, police sergeants, and post office managers.

What does this mean for selection and placement? Clearly, we must make a choice in placing managers or leaders. If we wish them to perform well immediately, we will need to choose people different from those we would choose for good performance eventually. We will need to take into consideration the personality of the individual, the degree to which the situation will provide the leader control and influence initially, and the degree of control likely in the more distant future. In organizations where most managers do not remain in the same job for more than a few years or where the need is for immediate performance, we shall wish to select those who will perform well with little or no experience. If the individual is expected to retain the job for a considerable time or if experience is readily gained in a short time, then we shall wish to select or assign on the basis of future performance requirements.

Training

The effects of leadership training are also predictable from the Contingency Model. Chemers, Rice, Sundstrom, and Butler conducted an experiment at the University of Utah in which ROTC students and psychology students were assembled into four-man teams. Half the groups had ROTC cadets with high LPC scores as leaders, and half had ROTC cadets with low LPC scores as leaders. These groups were then given random assignments. In one the leaders were given training in the task, how to decipher coded messages, while in the other the leaders were given irrelevant activities to fill their time.

All teams operated under a fairly high degree of stress and unpleasant interpersonal relations, and the position power of leaders was poor since they had no formal authority over their subordinates. Hence, leaders who were untrained and to whom the job was unstructured, would have very low situational control (cell 8 on Figure 2), and the task-motivated leaders should perform better than the relationship-motivated leaders. The trained leaders should have a structured task and, therefore, a moderate control situation (cell 6 in Figure 2). Hence, the relationship-motivated (high LPC) leaders should perform better than the task-motivated leaders.

That this actually did occur is shown in Figure 4. In addition, note that the task-motivated leaders with training not only performed less well than did the relationship-motivated leaders with training, but also less well than did the task-motivated leaders without training. We may assume, therefore, that the training actually *decreased* the performance of the task-motivated leaders. Informal observations of these groups showed that the task-motivated leaders were impatient with their group members, were bossy, and that there were disagreements among members of the groups which were headed by trained low LPC leaders.

Figure 4
INTERACTION OF TRAINING AND LPC ON GROUP PRODUCTIVITY

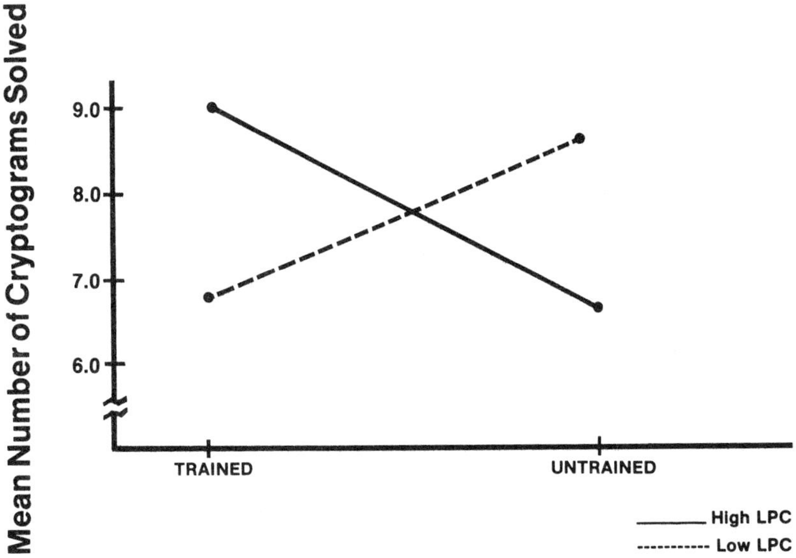

The Leader Match Program

According to the Contingency Model we can improve leadership performance either by changing the leader's motivation or by modifying the leadership situation so that it matches the leader's personality. Since it is much easier to change leadership situations than leader personality, the training program focuses on teaching the leader how to match the situation to his motivation. This training program—developed by Fiedler, Chemers, and Mahar—is called LEADER MATCH (*Improving Your Leadership Effectiveness: The Leader Match Concept*.)[3]

A self-administered programmed instruction workbook first enables individuals to identify their leadership motivation by completing an LPC scale. It then teaches them how to diagnose their situational control by using various scales. Finally, the individuals are taught how to modify the leadership situation to match their personality or motivational pattern.

Eight different validation studies of this program have now been conducted, four in civilian organizations and four in military settings. In each of the four civilian organizations, we obtained a list of leaders who were eligible for training. From this list we chose at random a group of those to be trained with *LEADER MATCH* and a group of controls who would receive no training. In the four civilian studies superiors subsequently rated the performance of all of their subordinates, usually without knowing whether a leader was in the trained or the control group. These ratings were obtained two to six months after training. Those studied were (a) personnel of a volunteer public health organization, (b) middle managers of a county government, (c) supervisors and managers of a public works department, and (d) sergeants of a police department. In each of these four studies, the trained leaders were rated as performing significantly and substantially better than the untrained leaders on such relevant items as effective management or use of information to make proper decisions.

Studies also were conducted under more highly controlled conditions at a naval air station and on a navy destroyer. Here again we obtained lists of eligible officers and petty officers. From these groups we chose at random a trained and a control group. Performance ratings were obtained at the time of training and again six months after training. Figure 5 shows the results for subjects in both studies. As can be seen, the trained group showed substantial and statistically significant improvement while the performance of the untrained group remained unchanged or slightly decreased. The decrease in the untrained group's performance probably reflects the fact that the improved performance of the trained leaders made the other leaders appear less effective in comparison.

Two other studies were conducted by Csoka and Bons with army personnel. These investigators worked with 154 officer candidates who were slated to serve as acting platoon leaders during the summer in various field units stationed throughout the United States. One third of this group was given the manual with instructions to read it before reporting to duty, one-third was informed of the design and purpose of the study, and one-third served as controls. At the end of the summer, these men were evaluated by their unit officers, who did not know that some individuals had received Leader Match training. As can be seen in Figure 6, trained leaders were rated as more effective than were the untrained leaders within the same unit.

In a second study, Csoka and Bons randomly selected, from each of 27 training companies, one of three platoon leaders to be given LEADER

Figure 5
MEAN PERFORMANCE OF TRAINED AND UNTRAINED LEADERS FROM A NAVY SHIP

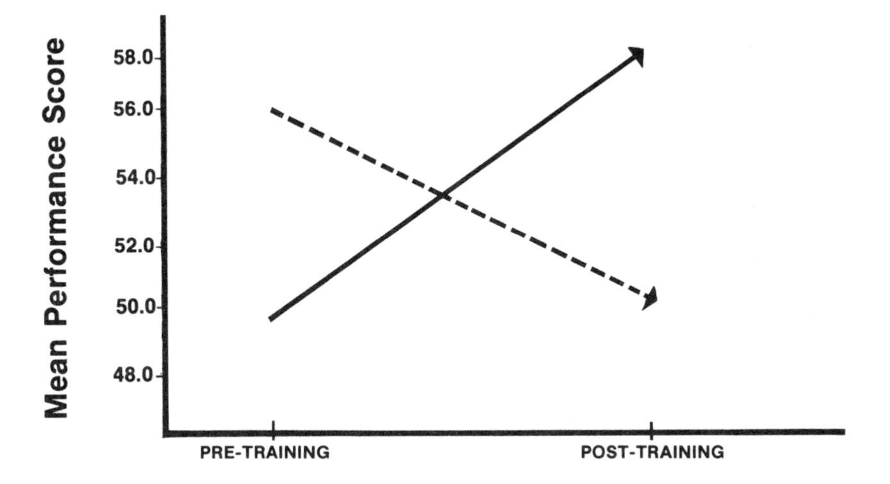

MEAN PERFORMANCE RATINGS FOR TRAINED AND UNTRAINED LEADERS

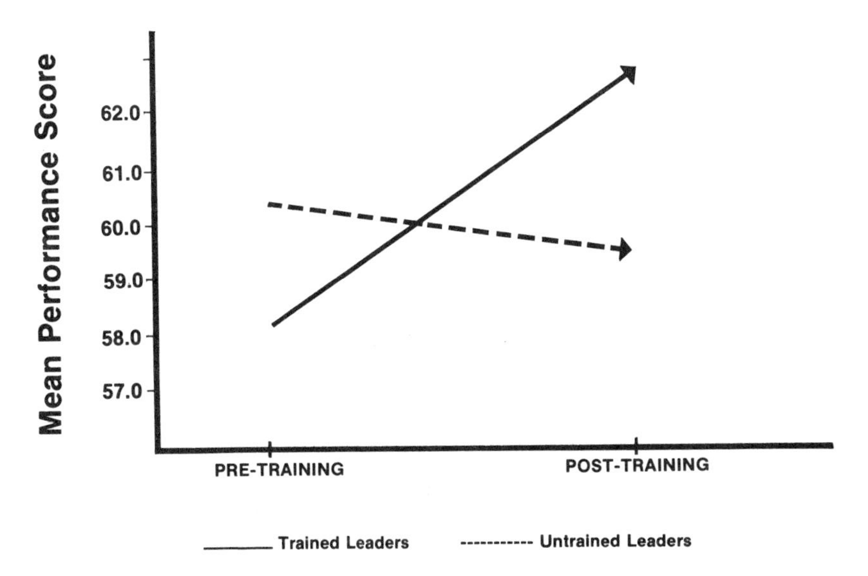

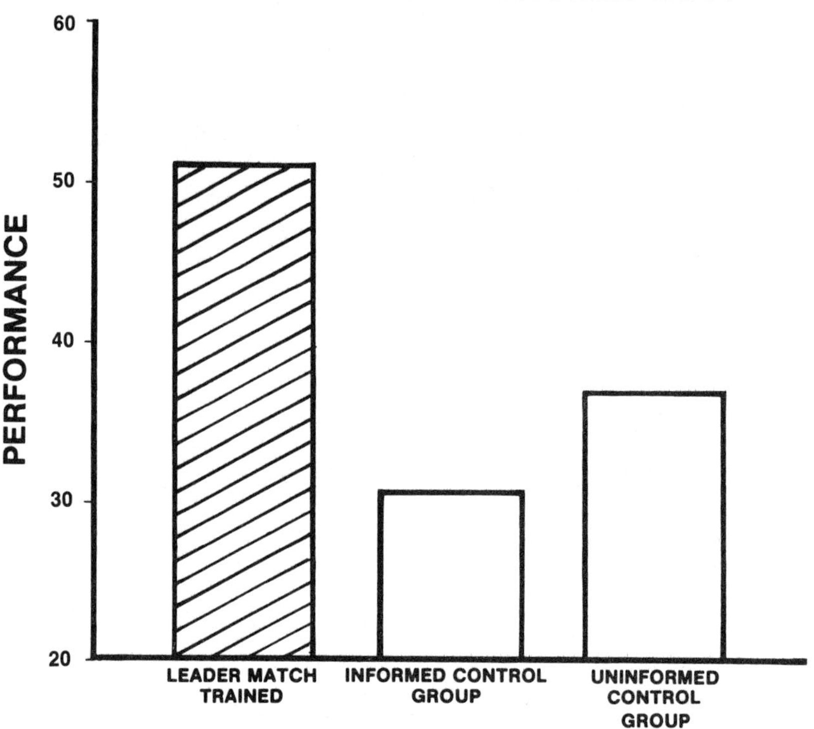

MATCH. At the end of the four-month period, all platoon leaders were rated on their performance. Those who had been trained were more frequently chosen as best or second best in their companies than were platoon leaders who had not been trained. This is shown in Figure 7 which indicates the number of platoon leaders with and without training who had been chosen as best, second best, or poorest in their company.

These eight studies on LEADER MATCH training—along with previous research on the effects of leader experience, training, and organizational turbulence—show that the concepts of the Contingency Model have broad implications for the management of leadership personnel and the better utilization of scarce managerial manpower. Leaders with an awareness of their own strengths and weaknesses, an understanding of the situations in which they perform well and poorly, and a set of tools for changing job situations to increase the match of self and

Figure 7
COMPARISON OF LEADER MATCH TRAINED AND UNTRAINED PLATOON LEADERS

	Rank Order*		
	1/3	2/3	3/3
Trained	14	4	8
Untrained	7	9	11

Chi Square 5.35 $p < .05$

* 1/3 = Best Platoon Leader of the Three in the Company
2/3 = Second Rated Leader
3/3 = Lowest Rated Leader in the Company

situation are likely to improve their own work and that of the organizations they serve.

NOTES

1. F. Fiedler, *A Theory of Leadership Effectiveness* Appendix D. (New York: McGraw-Hill, 1967).
2. *Ibid.*
3. F. Fiedler, M. Chemers, and M. Mahar, *Improving Your Leadership Effectiveness: The Leader Match Concept.* (New York: Wiley and Sons, 1976).

Part 2

POWER AND DECISION MAKING

Chapter 3

LEADER POWER

James A. Lee

When Harry Truman was President, he was asked by a reporter what he thought General Eisenhower would learn if elected president. Truman, sitting at his desk at the White House, answered: "For one thing, Ike will tell people to do this, do that, do this, and nothing will happen."[1] More recently Harlan Cleveland predicted that "What sets off the future executive from all previous generations is that he (and she) will be living in a society of which nobody can effectively be in charge."[2] Reflecting the same observations somewhat earlier, Eugene E. Jenning's first sentence in his 1960 book on leadership suggests that there can be no study of leadership since "Ours is a society without leaders."[3]

Alexander Butterfield, after 18 months as director of the U.S. Federal Aviation Authority, explained why he was having difficulty dealing with the agency's slow response to the need to exercise closer control over flight safety: "We're very institutionalized. . . . The cliques are fantastic. So much could be done but you need a free hand. I thought as an agency head you'd have clout. But you don't."[4]

The situation is no different in the field of education. Warren Bennis, former president of the University of Cincinnati, pointed up the many constraints on educational leaders. In referring to his increasing loss of autonomy, he pointed out that his hands were tied by governmental requirements (such as Affirmative Action), by litigation, by the moral—and sometimes legal—pressures of organized parents, consumers, and environmentalists. In addition to these external constraints, he noted that in vital decisions he had to consider not only students, faculty and administrators but also city councilmen, state legislators, the city manager, the governor, the federal government, as well as alumni and parents. He numbered the governance and interest groups monitoring and influencing his actions on his campus at over 500.[5]

The same shortage of leader clout also exists in business and industry. A new president of a large chemical company wanted to integrate what had been for years a group of semi-autonomous operating divisions. His background was in corporate finance and law, and he seldom traveled away from headquarters. In considering his power to bring about change, he should have taken into account his lack of adequate power to effectively decree integrative policy changes. His influence shortage was due largely to (a) the collective power of the division managers, (b) their expertise in the chemical production technology and marketing, (c) the legal powers resulting from their autonomous nature, and (3) the distance between him and the various division headquarters. His attempts at integration led to failure.

A general manager of a mining division of a major mining company oversaw an underground and an open pit operation, a primary crusher, a 27-mile company-owned railroad and a mill at the other end of the railroad. He was constantly plagued by a slow change rate at the mill. (His office was at the mine site.) Change and leader models rarely account for the reduction in the leader's power to influence, which in this case, was partly a simple matter of lack of physical proximity to his mill management. A further reduction in his power was due to subordinate expertise; his background was mining engineering, not chemical engineering. And the workers' collective power at the mill—he said they "always stick up for each other over there"—further reduced his influence. Or consider any foreman over a work group on a machine-paced assembly line where his subordinates are represented by a militant industrial union. All rewards and personnel policies of any consequence are determined by union and management negotiators, and the collective and legal powers of the foreman's workers are awesome. About all he has left in his power kit is his personality. The odds against his producing significant behavioral changes in his work group are astronomical.

In short, it seems evident that most leadership theories and models tend to ignore the various sources of power which largely determine the nature of the system in which the leadership model will be used.

To begin to deal with this costly oversight we need a power *system* approach to the study of leader power. Proposed here is a straight-forward analytic approach to taking an inventory of leader power. This approach requires an assessment of the leader's influence in the system after accounting for subordinate power, task design power, and extraneous power sources, all of which significantly limit leader influence. Such a power analysis approach can be used:

(1) *As a guide for an accurate inventory of leader power available to initiate change.* All too often change efforts bog down (as in the case of FAA Director Butterfield) because of vague assumptions about leader power available to change organizations and the behaviors of their members. These failures often muddy the waters so badly that the needed change is postponed further into the future than is necessary. (This need not be the case as we shall see later. Leader power can be enhanced in many situations to an adequate level for successful change management.)

(2) *As a means of realistically assessing performance of subordinate leaders.* Not infrequently, we expect subordinate managers and supervisors to perform as though there were few, if any, encroachments on their powers to get things done.

(3) *As an additional dimension to the assessment of organizational "health."* The West Coast shipping industry waited so long before such an inventory was taken that it cost millions to buy back the power to decide how their ships would be unloaded. An organization's ability to adapt to its changing environment can be impaired by the collective loss of its leaders' powers. If too much power has been lost, the rate at which leaders can initiate change for survival will be slowed.

It is true that a few theorists have noted variations in a leader's power in given situations. Fred Fiedler's leadership contingency model includes variables called "position power" (strong or weak), and "task structure" (high or weak), etc. Both the "Grid"[6] and "Life Cycle"[7] models call for a leader, in a given situation, to "initiate structure" but ignore the need for power in order to do this. Two popular change models—"unfreezing, change, refreezing" and the "force field"—focus mainly on the change processes and ignore the need for power to arrange for the unfreezing or to rearrange the forces against the planned change. More recent modelers include references to restrictions on leader power such as "organizational constraints" and "discretionary opportunities,"[8] to certain characteristics of task structures,[9] and to "macro" variables such as externally prescribed leader behaviors.

It seems reasonable that research on leader power may have been stunted by an over-focus on processes—group and change processes. Heller[10] pointed out that the focus on group processes has failed to reveal the full array of conditions under which managerial decisions are made. In his study of decisions made by 260 American managers, he found that managers relegated to low priority the use of participation in facilitating change. About one-half of their important decisions were made without consultation or participation. They saw participation as more important in subordinate training, subordinate satisfaction, and decision quality improvement than in facilitating change. Thus by focusing on *decisions* instead of *decisions made in groups*, Heller offered a clearer view of decision-making.

Some change management theorists, focusing more on the character of the internal change agent (respected, trusted, etc.), nevertheless see this person's power as an important ingredient in management of change.

> The persons being influenced need confidence that the change can, in fact be effected and a large part of this confidence comes initially from their confidence in the power and judgment of the influencing agent.[11]

In spite of numerous references to leader power in effecting change, none of the change models calls for taking a systematic power inventory before attempting organizational change. Such an inventory should probably be taken prior to selecting a change strategy, since strategies vary somewhat in the kinds of powers needed for their implementation.

A Leader Power System Inventory Model

The total power system approach offered here is as follows: total power affecting the subsystem equals leader power plus subordinate power plus work design power plus extraneous power, or

$$TP = LP + SP + WDP + EP$$

Solving for leader power:

$$LP = TP - (SP + WDP + EP).$$

In simple terms the leader power is what is left over after subtracting all types of subordinate power, various powers removed from the leader's control by the nature of the task and work environment, and that power removed by sources outside the subsystem. This approach permits a realistic analysis of various forces that affect a leader's ability to utilize any given change model.

Instinctively, we recognize that a supervisor over a group of Mexican-American farm workers in Arizona has more overall leader power than does a department chairman in a state university. Normally the same prescriptive leadership or change model would not be equally applicable to both. Again instinctively, a hospital administrator would not be expected to have as much leader power as the owner-manager of an advertising or auto agency. However, these crude distinctions are not based upon any real analysis, but such analyses could reveal the causes for many change effort shortcomings.

Power Sources

Leader Power—power theorists have noted that leader power is present in different forms:

1. *Position power* or legitimate power derives from the position of a leader in the organizational hierarchy because of ownership and/or appointment or election. It includes the power accruing from possession of information, veto powers, and power to set policy.
2. *Coercive power* is based upon the followers' fear of punishment and the leader's power to inflict it.
3. *Reward power* is based upon the followers' expectation of positive rewards and the leader's power to grant them.
4. *Expertise power* is derived from followers' and others' deference to the leader's special knowledge or skills.
5. *Referent* or *charismatic power* is based upon followers' and others' identification with the leader's personal traits or characteristics.

Proposition A: The greater the position power—coercive, reward, expertise, and/or referent—the more residual power available to him or her after power reduction from other sources has been accounted for.

Subordinate Power—There is no "classic list" of worker power sources; David Mechanic's listing is the most comprehensive. References to the erosion of management rights in the labor relations field are usually too general to be of model-building use, and leadership model builders tend to group them in different ways. Subordinates have powers and power opportunities from many sources. Some of the more important of these which can limit leader powers are:

1. *Collective power* derives from subordinates' membership in a union or informal association of workers which can collectively alter leader behavior or prevent the leader or the organization from reaching objectives.
2. *Legal powers* emanate from laws governing the treatment of employees or their associations regarding selection, hours, pay

rate, sex, national origin, religion, fringe benefits, and working conditions (safety and health).

3. *Referent* or *charismatic power* is based upon subordinates' influence on the leader, superiors, and co-workers owing to personal traits.
4. *Affluence power* derives from the reduction of subordinate economic dependence upon employing organizations. It is often exercised through subordinates' inclination to resist change or quit their jobs, and through absenteeism, tardiness, and threats to violate leaders' rules or company policy.
5. *Expert power* derives from leaders' and organizations' dependence upon subordinates' expertise, special skills, or knowledge. Included is power accruing to difficult-to-replace personnel.

Proposition B: The greater the collective, legal, affluence, charismatic, and expertise powers of the subordinates the less the total power available to the leader.

Consider the case of a brilliant systems engineer (Ph.D. EE) in a division of a major electronics company whose designs accounted for $15 million of the division's $65 million annual business. The company had a policy of paying for a maximum of two trips to meetings per year per engineer. Dr. Anton (not his real name) had already gone to two such meetings when he was invited to attend a worldwide symposium in Moscow. When asked by a friend if he planned to attend the meeting, he said, "Are you kidding? Of course I'm going, and on the company, too."

Work-Design Power—Beginning with the studies of Woodward, *et al.*,[12] research efforts have pointed toward the nature of the task as an important determinant of leader-followership systems. Although the majority of these studies were not directly aimed at measuring the effects of task technology on leader power, the implications from studies by House and Dessler, Stinson and Johnson, and Hunt and Osborn are that certain work designs do affect leader power. Some of the more significant categories of leader power-loss because of work design are:

1. *Engineered task-power* derives from the governance of subordinate and leader behavior by work design over which neither subordinate nor leader has direct control. Examples are machine-paced assembly lines, engineered assembly sequences, and production schedules set outside the production unit. If the job is routine and its components obvious to many workers, the opportunities for leader power through special knowledge or skill are severely reduced. Machine pacing and tight scheduling by

non-leaders limit the contact time available for the application and exercise of referent power. Since the opportunity to determine work goals and objectives is nearly eliminated, expertise power is reduced. The leader has little discretionary opportunity to initiate structure or consider subordinates' attitudes and ideas about work methods or objectives.

2. *Dispersed subordinates' work-design power* derives from the limitations of leader-follower interaction because of "distality" (lack of proximity) to each other. Some examples are dispersed plant managers, field geologists, international airline captains, territorial sales representatives, shovel runners in a large open pit, and supervisors reporting to a general supervisor who works a different shift.
3. *Over-the-leader's-head task power* derives from tasks whose approaches for accomplishment and possible outcomes are not fully understood by the leader. Interdisciplinary Research and Development projects and colleges with several academic disciplines under one head (Dean) illustrate situations in which collective expertise-powers limit the leaders' powers.

Proposition C: The more the subordinate task is structured by others, the more physically dispersed the subordinates, and the wider the variety of technical expertise required among subordinates, the less the total power available to the leader.

Extraneous Powers—The last locus of power which may rob the leader of power might be called extraneous (to the immediate leader-follower-technology subsystem) power. This power drain is derived from a wide variety of sources, of which a few are:

1. *Policy power* derives from the organization's policies and procedures that prescribe what leaders and workers must do in given situations. Policy powers seriously diminish the leader's power to assign, direct, decide, reward or punish. Not too many years ago some foremen could let an employee off work for personal reasons and decide whether his pay was to be docked. Today, many policy and procedure manuals specify in particular what the foreman's response to such a request must be.
2. *Organizational structure powers* are sources of power losses such as prescribed span of control, functional reporting relationships (to staff experts) and the nature of channels through which a leader must go to gain support, approvals, and instructions. Significant power is lost by a supervisor whose span is a prescribed 25 to 1 and who, before changing a production process, must

check with product planning, product engineering, and tool design, in addition to a line superior.

3. *The leader's superior's usurpation power* emanates from the leader's superior's power to withhold delegation of power to the leader and from circumventive communication and interaction between the leader's superior and the subordinates. The so-called "open door" policy, if not carefully administered, can encourage subordinates to go around their boss without his knowledge. This usually results in loss of power for the circumvented leader. And, of course, if a leader has a superior who goes directly to the leader's subordinates with tasks, instructions, etc., he will surely suffer a loss of power.
4. *Public-sentiment and interest-group powers* result from actual or threatened unofficial censure of leader behavior or pressures designed to control leader behavior and his decisions. Consider Warren Bennis' plight: " . . . I now have some 40 suits pending against the university, naming me as a defendant. I can no longer make even a trivial decision without consulting our lawyers. A woman who didn't work out in an administrative role is now suing me as, in effect, both a white racist and a male chauvinist, and I cannot either reply (except in court, say the lawyers) or sue for libel, since the Supreme Court has already held that public officials like myself cannot *be* libeled."[13] Not long ago in an Ohio town of 35,000 a hospital administrator fired his personnel manager and had to reverse that decision in the face of a citizens' group whose members were neither employees nor in any way associated with the hospital.

Proposition D: The greater the detail with which the organization's policies and procedures prescribe leader and subordinate behavior, the greater the detail with which the organizational structure and fixed reporting relationships are specified, the greater the circumventive interaction by subordinates and superiors, the greater the influence from outside the organization, the less the power available to the organization's leaders.

Practitioner Uses of the Model

The primary usefulness of the power inventory model for practitioners is in offering a more analytical approach to those who would improve their management of change. The model does not require personality structural changes on the leader's part nor alteration of organization structure.

Sensitivity training, grid training, or other such activities are not necessarily indicated. It does not suggest eliminating consideration of any of the various leader or change models. But its use may cause a leader attempting to initiate change to pause long enough to inventory the power available for influencing people toward the desired behavior. It may suggest that there are occasions when good temporary advice is "Don't just do something—stand there!" Yet the power-inventory approach does not necessarily suggest a "give-up" response when change is needed just because the inventory revealed a power shortage.

Central American Sugar Mill Case

Consider the case of the young newly hired Latin American sugar mill manager whose redesign of the production process altered the production workers' roles and pace considerably.[14] He was confronted with recalcitrant workers who were accustomed to high skill status and with orders from the owners not to fire anyone because a new labor law made discharge too costly. Close personal policing of the change during the first two months proved its economic value, but subsequent sabotage by worker resistance threatened the plant and his job. At this point, the power system model assesses the various powers in the system and shows why he was in trouble.

1. *Leader powers: Position power*—medium. (The owners left his non-technical powers relatively undefined.) *Coercive power*—low. (He was told these were limited to transfers to the undesirable milk-of-lime department.) *Reward power*—low. (He was told not to increase labor costs.) *Expertise power*—high. (He was a graduate engineer and had technical experience in another mill. *Referent power*—probably low. (He was 26 years old and half German; his mill workers averaged considerably older, especially the indigenous informal leaders.)
2. *Worker powers: Collective power*—considerable. (There was no union but they united behind an older worker who taught them their jobs and was leading the resistance to change.) *Legal power*—medium. (They believed the law would protect their jobs and behaved accordingly.) *Expertise power*—they believed it to be high. (They had learned the "art" of sugar—how to make it—not the science.) *Referent power*—medium to high. (A few indigenous leaders had considerable personal influence with the workers.)
3. *Nature of the task power: Work-design power*—high. (The process reduced the status of craftsmen and increased the work

pace; this stimulated the consolidation of workers' collective power.) *Worker dispersion*—medium. (Only one or two workers could be observed carefully by the manager at any one time.) *Over-the-leader's head power*—not applicable.

4. *Extraneous powers: Policy powers*—medium. (The owners insisted upon no discharges.) *Bosses' usurpation power*—limited his control by the policy powers above. *Public sentiment power*—negligible (except as expressed in the new labor law which placed a back-pay penalty for discharges for cause which were reversed by a government hearing body.)

From this simple inventory it becomes clear that the mill manager initiated the change without enough power to enforce the needed worker-behavioral change. The employees, working together, falsified reports in such a way that the real obstructionists were difficult to detect. When the manager finally identified the two indigenous leaders who apparently held most of the collective power of the mill workers, he was certain that the waters had been too muddied for rehabilitation. Recalling that he had been told by the owners not to fire anyone because of the labor laws, he went back to them—seeking more coercive power—and got their permission to see a lawyer about the possibility of firing the two recalcitrants. The lawyer explained that he could fire them on evidence of their refusal to follow operating instructions and of their falsifying records, provided he followed the warning notice procedures to the letter. He did so and successfully fired them. The mill began operating efficiently shortly thereafter.

The young mill manager went to his superiors for more power—coercive in this instance—to reduce the collective power of his subordinates. In the process, he discovered how to reduce the apparent legal powers of his subordinates to manageable proportions. His solution is not necessarily suggested as an ideal one. Had he taken a power inventory before instituting the change he might have noted the collective power held by a couple of the informal leaders of the mill workers. He might have been able to dilute or redirect this power by enlisting them as change agents, thereby avoiding the exercise of power which threatened to sabotage the effort.

U.S. Copper Mining Case

The mining company division general manager, mentioned earlier, who was plagued by a slow change rate at his mill, had a loss of power from several sources. His office at the mine site 27 miles away caused power loss through physical distance. He had come up through mining, not chemical engineering, losing some power through subordinate expertise, and the mill management was apparently a cohesive group which exercised certain collective powers. The division manager, however, undertook several moves designed to increase his influence over the mill management. He moved division headquarters to half-way between the mine and the mill, recovering some of the power lost through "distality." He centralized industrial relations and industrial engineering, thereby extending his position power more directly over the mill management. He could have gone further by adding to his office an assistant who was a chemical engineer, bringing a measure of expertise power to his office and thereby reducing the effective expertise power of the mill management.

The Chemical Company Case

Recall the earlier example of the chemical company president's failure to effect corporate integration? His power losses were from division managers' collective power, their expertise in the work technology, (his background was finance and law), and their division's legal entities. Had he taken a power inventory, several options for increasing his influence might have occurred to him. As in the case of the mining division manager, he could have added technological expertise to his office, perhaps by promoting people and using his ward power from the divisions. He could have formed a task force to accomplish the integration made up of the strongest division managers, thereby reducing the divisions' collective power and claiming some of their efforts for his objective. (Proponents of the "divide-and-conquer" approach certainly must have taken power inventories.) And, of course, he could have "gotten on his horse" and traveled more to the divisions to reduce the power lost through "distality."

The U.S. University President Case

A power inventory will not lead to miracles. Warren Bennis, as president of the University of Cincinnati, took a power inventory and found his office more or less powerless and resigned about a year later. A straightforward analysis of his situation would reveal few options expected to effectively restore power to the office of president. To reduce the non-leader powers in the system appears to be the only possible way to significantly increase the power of the president. A serious crisis, of course, has been known to rally divergent interest groups around a leader striving for the supraordinate goal of survival. But such events can rarely be created. Another option would be to eliminate structurally some of the legitimate powers of interest groups. In the case of the University of Cincinnati, this is what happened. Recall that Bennis named city councilmen and the city manager among those who must be considered before taking decisions? The basis for their influence has been considerably reduced since the state of Ohio took over the university, making it into another state university. A number of the interest groups had to restructure their roles to fit the bureaucracy of the state university system. On a temporary basis, this restructuring offers some reduction of the non-leader powers in the system. The outcome will depend upon the new leader's ability and willingness to collect all the power available and use it to lead the institution.

The Case of the American Factory Foreman

In 1945 (and again as a classic in 1965) the *Harvard Business Review* published Fritz Roethlisberger's article "The Foreman: Master and Victim of Double Talk." Roethlisberger described in some detail the foreman's loss of power over a 25-year period (1920-1945):

> To the foreman it seems as if he is being held responsible for functions over which he no longer has any real authority. For some time he has not been able to hire and fire and set production standards. And now he cannot even transfer employees, adjust the wage inequalities of his men, promote deserving men, develop better machines, methods and processes, or plan the work of his department, with anything approaching complete freedom of action. All these matters for which he is completely or partially responsible have now become involved with other persons and groups, or they have become matters of company policy and union agreement. He is hedged in on all sides with cost standards, production standards, quality standards, standard methods and procedures, specifications, rules, regulations, policies, laws, contracts, and agreements; and most of them are formulated without his participation.[15]

If anything, the picture is bleaker today, over three decades later. His subordinates' powers—collective, legal, and affluence—have surely increased since 1945. Methods and process engineers have certainly not been idle since 1945. And policy and procedure manuals as well as union-management agreements have grown thicker each year, adding to constraints on the foreman. A brief look at the inventory model offers few suggestions for increasing his powers. On the national front a few gains are being made. Unions are winning fewer elections, and OSHA inspectors can no longer invade the factory floor unannounced without a filed complaint. But on the factory floor, it would appear that outside of his charismatic or referent powers (and little can be done in the short range to jazz up his personality), the only course would be for management to give back to him some of the powers they have themselves taken away. If his stand-up desk on the factory floor can be improved to a semi-private cubicle; if he can be trained to interpret more policy to inquiring employees; if he receives proper *staff* assistance with grievance decisions as well as good line advice several grievance steps up, thereby reducing reversals of his decisions; if he is given more information about the company itself—its prospects, plans, objectives—so that he can be a ready and reliable source of information for his people; if a management sets out to do all these things, first-line supervisors will gain in power and can be expected to supervise more effectively.

Management's failure to note and do something about the frustrations resulting from the victimization described in Roethlisberger's article has led to an increasing turn-down rate of foreman promotional offers. In some major companies in the mid-west, the rate is as high as 50%. Unless there is considerable and serious concern on American industrial management's part, the first line leader, an extremely important managerial team member, will be lost with consequent productivity losses.

Summary and Conclusions

Today's leaders are losing power at an increasing rate. Part of the reason for this is due to a form of managerial "ostrichism" about the sources of power. Once the powers have been carefully identified and their strengths assessed, a plan is possible to add to leaders' powers by arranging for realignment of some of the powers in the system. Fretful references to the erosion of management rights do not help simply because they are vague laments—not based on analyses. Hoping for an increase in the proportion of charismatic leaders willing to take bolder risks has no basis in modern industrial societies. They are being culturally bred out. But there are many power sources in leadership-followership-technology systems, and some of them, in many cases enough, can be shifted to enhance leader powers sufficiently for producing the necessary organizational and behavioral change required for institutional survival and growth.

NOTES

1. Richard E. Neustadt, *Presidential Power* (New York, N. Y.: Wiley, 1964), p. 22.
2. Harlan Cleveland, "Systems, Purposes, and Watergate," *Operations Research* (September-October, 1973), p. 1021.
3. Eugene E. Jennings, *An Anatomy of Leadership* (New York, N. Y.: McGraw-Hill, 1960), p. xv.
4. "A Need to Get 'Tough as Hell,' " *Time*, December 23, 1974, p. 31-32.
5. Warren Bennis, "Managing the Unmanageable," *The Chronicle of Higher Education* (September 22, 1975), p. 20.
6. R. R. Blake and J. S. Mouton, *The Managerial Grid* (Houston: Gulf Publishing Company, 1964).
7. Paul Hersey and Kenneth Blanchard, *Management of Organizational Behavior* (Englewood Cliffs, N. J.: Prentice-Hall, 1972)

8. Bernard M. Bass and Enzo R. Valenzi, "Contingent Aspects of Effective Management Styles," In James G. Hunt and Lars L. Larson, (Eds.) *Contingency Approaches to Leadership* (Carbondale, Ill.: Southern Illinois University Press, 1974), pp. 130-155.

9. R. J. House and G. Dessler, "The Path-Goal Theory of Leadership: Some *Post Hoc* and *A Priori* Tests," in J. G. Hunt and L. L. Larson (Eds.) *Contingency Approaches to Leadership* (Carbondale, Ill.: Southern Illinois University Press, 1974).

10. Frank A. Heller, *Managerial Decision-Making* (London: Tavistock, 1971).

11. Gene W. Dalton, "Influence and Organizational Change," in Gene W. Dalton, Paul R. Lawrence, and Larry E. Greiner, *Organization Change and Development* (Homewood, Ill.: Richard D. Irwin, 1970).

12. Joan Woodward *et al., Industrial Organizations: Theory and Practice* (London, Oxford Univerity Press, 1965), p. 74.

13. Warren Bennis, *op. cit.*, p. 20.

14. "El Gallito Sugar Mill," Case registered with Harvard Case Clearing House.

15. Fritz J. Roethlisberger "The Foreman: Master and Victim of Double Talk," *Harvard Business Review*, Spring 1945, pp. 288.

Chapter 4

A MULTIPLE-INFLUENCE APPROACH TO LEADERSHIP FOR MANAGERS[1]

J. G. Hunt

R. N. Osborn

The scene is the White House. It is the time of the Cuban missile crisis. The President of the United States is trying to lead our country out of this dilemma. Most people would probably consider him to be the most powerful man in the United States, if not the world. Thus, at first blush it might be argued that he would have almost unlimited control over his leadership options.

Yet, this was far from the case. In actuality, he faced a number of constraints and pressures which restricted his leadership behavior. First, he was still feeling the backlash from the unsuccessful Bay of Pigs invasion attempt. Second, there was a traditional lack of concern among Organization of American States members with the threat of communism. The third concern was the presence of an American naval base at Guantanamo and Jupiter satellites in Italy and Turkey. As suggested by von Petterffy and Diamond, all of these and more served as constraints on the President's leader behavior.[2]

If the President of the U.S. is so restricted, what about a manufacturing supervisor on a mechanized assembly line or an elected chairman of a voluntary committee? Are there some organizations or situations that control or restrict a leader's behavior more than others? It would seem so; yet we hardly know. And this admission is in spite of the recent emphasis on so-called "contingency" or situational leadership approaches. These approaches tell managers to alter their leadership to the group they supervise or the individual personality characteristics of subordinates.[3] We think contingency models are a step in the right direction. They are much more sophisticated than earlier directives which admonished leaders merely to be expert in human relations or expert in both human relations and task-structuring behaviors.[4] However, we also think additional considerations need to be emphasized.

First, the organizational setting in which the leader and his subordinates are embedded needs to be considered in some detail. Picking out one or two variables within the setting and then estimating the manner in which these alter the impact of leadership is just too simplistic. A model of leadership should recognize the complexity of the organizational setting within which leaders and subordinates function.

Second, some leaders have more clout than others. A model of leadership should help the manager identify opportunities for leadership. It should help steer him away from wasting his time and effort if improved performance or satisfaction cannot be obtained via better leadership. Better leadership is not *the* answer to all problems.[5]

At the same time, in most existing leadership models, it is as if leadership springs full-blown from the earth. Yet, as already suggested, it is likely that the organizational setting will affect both the amount and kind of leadership open to the manager. In some cases, his behavior toward subordinates will be highly circumscribed; in other cases, he will have almost unlimited discretion. An approach to leadership is needed which recognizes the potential differences in discretion which different settings provide the leader.

Finally, existing models treat leadership as an influence process directed toward *either* a group or individual. The contingency theory first proposed by Fred Fiedler, for instance, deals with leadership at the group level (See Fiedler's article in this volume for the latest restatement of this approach). On the other hand, some recent models treat leadership at the individual or one-on-one level.[6] Since many, if not most, leadership theorists are also psychologists or trained by psychologists, much of the leadership literature concentrates on the one-on-one relationship between a leader and a subordinate. We contend that managers use both group and one-on-one leadership. The trick is to know what mix is likely to yield the best results. A leadership model is needed which focuses on this issue.

This article sketches a framework which considers the above issues. It incorporates the notions that the organizational setting within which the leader and subordinates must operate is important, that some leaders have more clout than others, that leadership is only in part self-determined, and that managers use both group and one-on-one influence attempts. These multiple considerations suggest the title for our framework—"a multiple-influence approach to leadership."

First, the overall multiple-influence framework and its key components are described at a very general level. Then we examine the major components of the approach in greater detail to derive some practical implications for the practicing manager. Specifically, what leadership strategy should the manager take? When should effort be expended to change leadership? When might it be better to alter the setting? There are no simple answers. We don't promise that with our approach, performance and satisfaction will miraculously increase. But, we do think the approach makes practical sense, fits with the experience of many managers, and has the potential to open some previously neglected directions.

Highlights of a Multiple-Influence Approach

Since there are probably as many definitions of leadership as there are leadership theorists, we need to define what we mean by leadership. To us, leadership is the influence attempt a superior makes toward his subordinates as a group or on a one-on-one basis.

The heart of our approach is the difference between what we call discretionary and nondiscretionary leadership. Discretionary leadership is that initiated by the leader himself. Nondiscretionary leadership, on the other hand, is that dictated by environment, organization, and group variables in the leader's organizational setting. That is, discretionary leadership is under the leader's volition while nondiscretionary leadership is leader behavior invoked by the setting. Assume for a moment that a leader is breathing down an employee's neck. This close supervision may be primarily dictated by his organizational setting (nondiscretionary leadership) or it may take place primarily because that is the leader's natural predisposition (discretionary leadership).

What does the successful leader do? Essentially, we see him as filling the gap between subordinate desires and abilities on one hand and organizational goals and requirements on the other. In essence, when the gap is filled, there should be satisfied subordinates in a high performance organization. The leader can fill this gap by exerting leadership influence at two levels either singly or in combination. The first of these is for the group as a whole via group meetings, emphasis on committees, etc. The second is by one-on-one contact with various individuals within the group.

The leader's ability to fill the gap is affected by the setting within which he operates. When environment and organization variables are complex and group variables are unfavorable, two things occur. First, the gap widens and calls for more active leadership intervention. Second, at the very time a leader's influence is most needed, the complexity and unfavorableness cut his discretion. Let's examine these highlights in more detail to gain a better understanding of them.

Leadership and the Organizational Setting

What are the factors in the setting which cut discretion and widen the gap? In addition to group variables, to be discussed later, the organizational literature suggests four.[7] These are environmental complexity, management philosophy, technological complexity, and structural complexity.

Environmental Complexity

The external environment of the organization becomes more complex as that organization becomes more dependent upon others, finds the actions of other organizations more uncertain or difficult to predict, and experiences a decline in external opportunities.[8] Increasing dependency upon other units reduces the autonomy of the organization and its leaders and forces the incorporation of the desires of external units into decision making. Uncertainty undercuts the ability of the organization and its leaders to establish control and continuity in internal operations and thus increases inconsistency in decision making. Declining external opportunities cut the resources available to leaders to exchange with subordinates. In other words, a leader's discretionary behavior potential is reduced and nondiscretionary leadership becomes a larger proportion of the leader's behavior.[9] For example, a leader in a small firm, ninety percent of whose output goes to two large firms which are themselves subject to unpredictable demand swings in a declining industry, would have fewer leadership options than he would in a more favorable environment.

Management Philosophy

Another important variable is the philosophy of top management.[10] Management philosophy may be considered as reactive or proactive.[11] A reactive philosophy is characterized by action which post-dates changes in environmental conditions or performance. A proactive management strategy is characterized by action in anticipation of environment or organizational changes.

A reactionary philosophy of top management may cut lower level discretion by restricting options. There may be insufficient time for adequate planning or thorough analysis of problems. The more important impact, however, is likely to occur in combination with increasing environmental complexity. A reactive strategy in combination with increasing environmental complexity is likely to all but eliminate lower-level discretion. Managers are up to their ears in alligators trying continually and rapidly to adjust without adequate planning. Thus, the decrease in lower level discretion owing to environmental complexity is reinforced, rather than offset, by a reactive philosophy.

Technological Complexity

Technology is more complex the higher the required skill level of subordinates, the less the predictability, and the greater the dependence of one subsystem upon another. These notions are borrowed from Melcher and bear an obvious similarity to those defining environmental complexity.[12]

As the skill required to successfully complete an operation increases, subordinates, not leaders, are in a position to dictate outcomes. And, just as technological uncertainty and interdependence are similar to environmental uncertainty and interdependence, so too is their effect on discretion. As technology becomes more complex, leader discretion is decreased. For example, the leader of a group of highly sophisticated metallurgists working to develop the front half of a moon rocket housing would have less discretionary leadership available than he would under a less complex technology.

Organization Structure Complexity

The organizational literature suggests that delegation, formalization, and departmentation, at least, are important components of structural complexity.[13] A complex structure is considered to be one with: (1) a low degree of delegation (a centralized authority structure); (2) a high degree of formalization (heavy reliance on rules, policies and procedures); and (3) functional (highly interdependent) as opposed to autonomous departmentation. Burns and Stalker would term this a mechanistic rather than an organic organization.[14]

Each of these characteristics decreases a leader's discretion. Centralized authority takes away lower level discretion since managers merely implement the decisions of superiors. Formalization cuts discretion by dictating standardized procedures. Functionally interdependent departments cut discretion in much the same way as do environmental and technological dependency. The head of a unit in the middle of an interdependent workflow has less discretion, for example, than the leader of a unit at either the beginning or end of the workflow, where the interdependence is less.

Fit Among Environmental and Organizational Conditions

Environmental and organizational conditions alter leader discretion and the subordinate-organization gap directly as described above. But, the leader faces all of these in combination. Literature on the combined impact of environmental and organizational conditions suggests that the fit (or lack of fit) among these variables is likely to be important.[15] Extending Thompson's ideas we see that complexity in the environment can be offset via a more proactive management philosophy, a less complex technology, and/or a less complex structure.[16] Typically, the technology employed by the organization is fixed or becoming more complex. If not offset by a more proactive management philosophy or less complex structure, leader discretion, we speculate, is likely to diminish as the technology becomes more sophisticated. While we would like to be able to be more specific in this arca, not enough research is yet available to say more.

Group Variables

So far, we have acted as if a leader's discretion were determined entirely by environmental and organizational aspects of the setting. However, not all groups face environmental and organizational pressures to the same degree. Some may be relatively isolated from complex environmental pressures or so far removed from top management that its philosophy has little impact. Furthermore, group variables themselves can provide a leader with alternative sources of discretion.

What then are some important group variables which allow the leader to build discretionary influence? While there are probably a number of these, a key one at this stage of development of the multiple-influence framework appears to be group cohesiveness *and* the extent to which group member and organizational goals are congruent. A cohesive and hostile group can offset the environmental and organizational discretion provided the leader. Rewards at the leader's disposal are of little use if a cohesive group rejects them. On the other hand, a cohesive group which has goals congruent with those of the organization provides additional discretion for the leader. In effect, the group is ready to go to work and to be positively influenced by the leader.

The size of the group also appears to have a direct bearing on the discretion available to the leader. Very simply, the larger the group, the less discretion. As the size of the unit grows, the leader finds it more difficult to get all subordinates together and finds less time available for one-on-one interface with each subordinate. Figure 1 summarizes the major components of our multiple-influence approach.

Figure 1
MAJOR COMPONENTS OF THE MULTIPLE INFLUENCE APPROACH TO LEADERSHIP

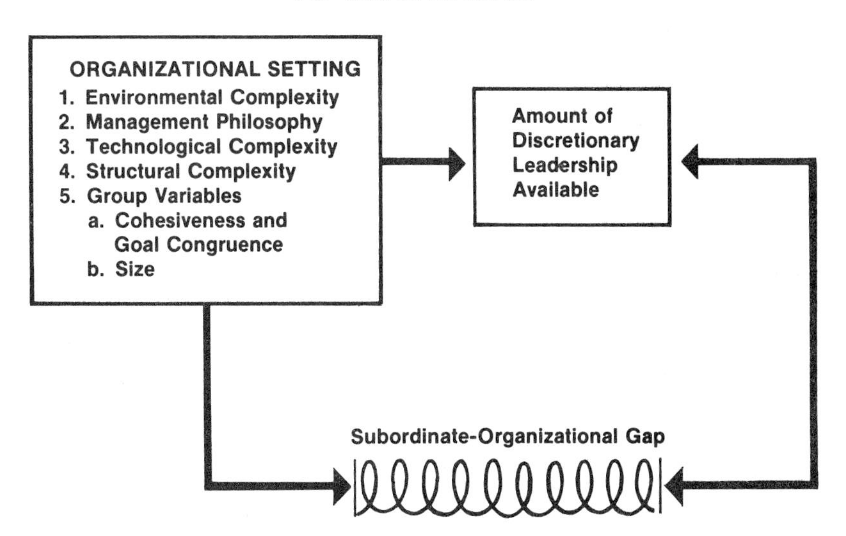

The Mix of Group and One-on-One Leadership

Now we are ready to look at a key strategic leadership choice. What mix of group and one-on-one leadership should be used? We cannot, at this stage of development of our approach, provide specific recommendations. We can, however, provide some considerations which we believe are important. These considerations are based on the assumption that the more favorable the conditions facing the leader, the less powerful the effect of subordinate, individual-personality variables. The same variables which affect leader discretion are assumed to have a direct impact on subordinate satisfaction and opportunities for growth and development. For example, when there is a rich and unlimited supply of food on the table, it makes little difference whether those at the table are aggressive or retiring, introverted or extroverted; all can be taken care of. But, when the supply becomes short, individual characteristics will come to the forefront.

At least three factors appear important in deciding upon the mix of group and one-on-one leadership. They are (1) the amount of discretion available to the leader, (2) the nature of the group being supervised, and (3) subordinate characteristics.

The Mix and the Amount of Discretion

Other things equal, the more discretion available to the leader, the more emphasis that should be placed on group-influence attempts. At the very time the leader's discretion is the highest, the environment and organization variables enhance the probability of group receptiveness. Group-influence attempts help build group cohesiveness and reinforce the natural tendency of the group to adopt informal norms, values, and sentiments which are consistent with the desires of management. A leader with little discretion, on the other hand, is more likely to encounter an unresponsive, and perhaps even hostile, group. If he confronts the group without considerable discretion, he only reinforces the negative effects of environmental and/or organizational conditions. He is probably better off if he emphasizes one-on-one leadership. At least here he can respond to the concerns of an employee directly.

In an extremely unfavorable situation, it is unlikely that either group or one-on-one leadership will close the subordinate-organization gap. The leader's discretionary behavior is just too circumscribed. The group and its members are too unresponsive.

The Mix and the Nature of the Group

First to be considered is the size of the group. The larger the group, the more the leader is forced into using group leadership if for no other reason than that time does not permit a heavy one-on-one emphasis. However, the leader may focus one-on-one influence attempts on the informal leader (s) as a back-up to group leadership. This focusing of one-on-one leadership can provide the leader with valuable feedback concerning the impact of his actions and the reaction of individuals to environmental and organizational conditions.

We have argued that a cohesive but hostile group cuts discretion. The leader with little clout should probably not confront a cohesive/hostile group directly. Instead, he should emphasize one-on-one leadership to help cut group cohesiveness or at least to avoid reinforcing existing group patterns. Quite the opposite is the case when the group is cohesive and shares goals congruent with those of management. The leader has a team ready to accept his group leadership and he should use this opportunity to increase satisfaction and productivity.

Obviously, the social aspect of the group is only part of the picture. The task the group must perform is important, and the leader should probably adjust the mix of group and one-on-one leadership to recognize such importance. More specifically, the literature suggests that at least task predictability and interdependence are likely to be important.[17] The less the predictability of the task, the more one-on-one leadership is likely to be needed to reduce uncertainty and to allow the leader to show the path toward successful task accomplishment. And as the jobs of group members become more interdependent, the leader should probably shift the mix toward group leadership. Coordination and pacing among subordinates is critical and can be more easily accomplished with group-influence attempts. With high task interdependency, the leader's job is much like balancing an integrated assembly line. Where tasks are both unpredictable and highly interdependent, interdependency should probably be weighed more heavily in determining the mix between group and one-on-one leadership than task predictability.

The difference between technology and task, as the terms are used here, should be specified. Technology is considered to be the work flow between units or subsystems; task is considered to be the workflow facing individuals within each unit. A worker may face a situation where both technology and task have similar characteristics (in terms of dependence and predictability) or where they are quite different from each other. Our arguments in this section assume similarity. Where technology and task are dissimilar, the leader faces conflicting pressures which may make his position so difficult that neither group nor one-on-one leadership can be effectively used.

The Mix and Subordinate Characteristics

There are probably a whole host of individual, subordinate variables which could be important here. For example, a subordinate's experience and where he fits into the group are likely to be important. Inexperienced workers probably need as heavy a dose of one-on-one leadership as do individuals who are not accepted by the group. The new worker is likely to need the leader as a guide to the new job. The deviant needs the leader's social support. We stress these two subordinate characteristics primarily because they are easily detected by managers and readily fit into our overall scheme. The underlying attitudes and values of individuals—the need for autonomy, subscription to the Protestant work ethic, and professionalism—may also be important. Incorporation of variables such as these into our framework, however, awaits results based on the present variables.

Summary

To summarize we repeat that the amount of leadership discretion, the nature of the group, and subordinate characteristics are believed to be important determinants of the most effective mix between group and one-on-one leadership. When we know more about how setting variables fit together and more about the relative importance of various individual characteristics, we can be more specific in our recommendations. We should also reiterate the earlier point that there are times *when neither group nor individual leadership will have much impact.* And, again, we refer to Kerr's interesting work which is related to but somewhat different from ours.[18]

What Kind of Leader Behaviors?

Common sense and the leadership literature suggest that leader behavior can be divided into a number of separate dimensions. Assuming the leader has an idea of the desired mix of group and individual leadership, then which of these specific leadership dimensions should be emphasized? Two such dimensions, consideration and initiating structure, have received the most attention in the leadership literature and will be considered here.[19] Consideration refers to socio-emotional or human-relations-influence attempts on the part of the leader while initiating structure centers on directing subordinates in the what and how of task accomplishment. A third dimension, called lateral relations, will also be discussed since it is a method of increasing leader discretion. Lateral relations center on the interactions between a leader and those at or near his own organizational level, *outside* his own chain of command.

Recent literature suggests that initiating structure or similar behavior reduces task-related uncertainty.[20] Thus, at the group level, structure can be used to increase coordination by planning. At the individual level, it clarifies how an individual should act and how his job should be performed. Initiating structure can also reduce task complexity by detailing exactly how the work is to proceed. Lastly, it can be used to specify the priority of quality versus quantity.

Consideration can be used in three related ways. First, people like compliments and kind words whether they relate to job performance or not. (However, Hunt and Osborn suggest that consideration may have a more positive impact if it is not used too indiscriminantly.[21] This is called the "manure hypothesis." Up to a point, the more the better. But beyond that point, indiscriminate use may "stink" or at least not help very much.)

Second, at the group level, consideration provides social support to reinforce current group actions and norms. At the individual level, it reassures the subordinate that in a complex organization at least one manager knows he is an individual with a number of important roles. "How are the wife and kids?" "How is Ruth coming with her new courses and is Johnny still doing well on the swimming team?" "Your bowling score was down last night, I hear."

Third, consideration can be a form of recognition and reinforcement for a job well done. For instance, putting suggestions of the group into operation recognizes the group's past accomplishments and successes. At the individual level, it may be one of the few rewards open to some supervisors.[22]

The leader's emphasis upon these dimensions depends upon the nature of the subordinate-organization gap. For instance, it is expected that if uncertainty is widening the gap between subordinate desires and management expectations, initiating structure will be more helpful than consideration. However, if employees cannot get individual rewards for successful task accomplishment, then consideration should be employed. While such recommendations are not as specific as we might like, they become more meaningful when the lateral-relations dimension is also considered.

These "exchanges" between a leader and those at or near his own organizational level, outside his own chain of command, are quite important but often neglected. While we call this aspect of leadership "lateral relations," perhaps a more common term is "politics."[23] Regardless of the label used, these exchanges can build discretion by providing a more consistent flow of varied resources, reducing uncertainty and/or increasing independence or autonomy.

Lateral relations are particularly important when the other sources of discretion are at a minimum. Suppose, for example, that there is an electronics firm with a highly mechanistic structure and a highly complex technology. To respond to fast changing market conditions, the head of marketing engages in lateral relations with the head of research and development. In this way, the marketing leader may compensate for the excess complexity and slowness in responding to market conditions and may help build discretion within his own unit.

Lateral relations can also be used to trade an overabundance of one type of organizational resource for a broader mix of resources. For instance, if the leader has excess labor, he may "allow" a subordinate to help an adjacent group in return for help in the future. This strategy is particularly useful where discretion is cut by rapidly changing environmental demands which place an imbalanced demand on different units. Via cooperative action, all leaders may be able to increase their discretion.

We also suspect that lateral relations may not be used at the very time they are most needed. When the discretion of the leader is low, he has less bargaining room with other units and must trade future benefits for immediate help. Superiors can be particularly helpful in this situation by informally ratifying lateral exchange arrangements and cooperative action.

The movie and book *The Godfather* provide additional insight into the value of these exchange relationships.[24] At one point, the Godfather is approached by an undertaker whose daughter has been assaulted by two men. The undertaker reported the assault to the police, and the judge sentenced the men and then let them go on probation. The Godfather agrees to "handle" the situation to provide "justice" for the undertaker. The Godfather indicates that sometime in the future, the undertaker may have to repay his debt. Repayment is made when one of the Godfather's sons is killed and bady mauled in a gang war. The undertaker takes over the body and spends great effort to make it presentable. Sometimes, this kind of exchange is called the "norm of reciprocity."[25] An individual does a favor for another, creating an obligation which must be reciprocated at an appropriate future time.

Discretionary and Nondiscretionary Leadership Revisited

So far, we have implied that a leader who was high on nondiscretionary behavior would have to be low on discretionary behavior or vice versa. While this may frequently be true, it does not have to be. For instance, it is likely, in many cases, that a leader may display roughly equal amounts of each kind of behavior. Here, an important consideration is the combination of discretionary and nondiscretionary leadership. It may be possible either to reinforce or counter nondiscretionary behavior with discretionary behavior. For example, if the setting requires rigid enforcement of rules via close supervision, the leader may be able to soften rigidity by discretionary consideration.

It is an oversimplification to presume that all leaders will utilize the discretionary behavior open to them. There are at least three leader characteristics which will affect the use of discretion. The first are the leader's task and human relations skills. If the leader doesn't know how to structure subordinate activities, is not adept at interpersonal relations, or is uncomfortable confronting a group, he will display less discretionary leadership.

Second, leaders who see opportunities for the development and use of discretion are more likely to use discretionary leadership. In more technical terms, a leader's internal versus external locus of control may be important.[26] It seems likely that leaders who think events are primarily dictated by forces outside their control will be less willing to use discretionary leadership, other things being equal.

Third, even if a leader is skillful and sees discretionary leadership opportunities, he may still be unwilling to utilize discretionary leadership. Miner and his associates have identified a complex of attitudinal variables called "motivation to manage" which appear relevant.[27]

Those with more "motivation to manage" more readily accept management objectives, compete for resources, assert their desires over others, assume authority over groups, and accept more responsibility than individuals with a lower motivation to manage. We propose that as the "motivation to manage" increases, a leader will exert more discretionary behavior, other things being equal.

Leadership Training Versus Organizational Design

We have spun out a tentative and elaborate approach to leadership based on multiple influence. What are some of the implications of this framework for leadership training? First, leadership training cannot be divorced from organizational design since the nature of the organization has a direct impact on leadership. If leadership is primarily nondiscretionary, traditional leadership training, in which an attempt is made to change the leader's behavior, will be a waste of time and money. Campbell, Dunnette, Lawler, and Weick and Hunt, among others, have shown that leadership training programs have typically not been very successful.[28] Fiedler and Chemers argue that one of the reasons may be that leaders with diametrically opposite leadership styles are given the same training and, thus, what might be appropriate for one is not successful for the other.[29] Our framework suggests another view. Namely, that much training may have been directed toward: (1) behaviors which were nondiscretionary, or (2) toward changing attitudes in hopes of a behavior change which, in reality, is not available to the trainees (*e.g.*, making them human-relations oriented so they will be more considerate when their job duties will not allow time for consideration). Such training may even be dysfunctional if it raises a leader's hopes of changing conditions back on the job when, in fact, he cannot. Such a leader may think there is something wrong with him when, in actuality, his setting is to blame.

While the above kind of training is not appropriate for nondiscretionary leadership, diagnostic training does appear to be. Specifically, the leader can be trained to determine the mix of discretionary leadership to accompany nondiscretionary behavior and to utilize the mix of group and one-on-one leadership most appropriate to the setting. Further, the leader could be coached in lateral relations to help identify others at his level who would be willing to develop mutually rewarding exchange relationships.

If an alteration in the direction open to leaders is desired, organizational design changes may be considered. It might be possible to change some of the variables in the setting to provide more or less discretionary leadership. For instance, structural complexity might be reduced to enhance leadership discretion. If subordinate leaders are exercising too much discretion, just the opposite might be instituted. Or, when the organization's structure is being changed, consideration may be given as to how such alterations will open or close areas of discretion for lower level managers.

Organizational design and leadership training might be considered together. For instance, management might be committed to a program of job enrichment by altering the complexity of employee tasks. Leadership training might be considered to help managers adjust to these changes in their leadership setting.

These and other possibilities are suggested by our multiple-influence approach to leadership. It remains for us to refine it by incorporating the critical comments of scholars and practitioners and by testing it empirically. We think the approach highlights some neglected theoretical and practical concerns.

Is the multiple-influence approach useful as it stands? Think about it before starting an expensive training program. Think about it before condemning the poorly performing manager. Maybe he doesn't have the discretion to change his subordinates. Think about it before promoting a successful manager. Can he take advantage of the additional discretion in the new position? Finally, think about it when considering group versus one-on-one leadership or using lateral relations to help strengthen individual discretion.

NOTES

1. Thanks are due to David A. Gray, Lee Hendrick, Larry O. Secrest, and John E. Stinson for helpful comments on an earlier draft.

2. G. A. von Petterffy & S. L. Diamond, "Power and Decision Making in the Cuban Missile Crisis." Intercollegiate Case Clearing House, Harvard Business School, ICH14G33, 1970.

3. F. E. Fiedler, M. M. Chemers & P. M. Bons, "Implications of the Contingency Model for Improving Organizational Effectiveness," this volume; and R. J. House & T. R. Mitchell, "Path-Goal Theory of Leadership," this volume.

4. (See L. L. Larson, J. G. Hunt & R. N. Osborn, "The Great *Hi-Hi* Leader Behavior Myth: A Lesson from Occam's Razor," *Academy of Management Journal*, 1976, *19*, 628-641, for a review).

5. S. Kerr, "Substitutes for Leadership: Their Meaning and Measurement." *Organizational Behavior and Human Performance*, in press, also makes a similar argument though from a somewhat different perspective.

6. G. Graen & J. F. Cashman, "A Role-Making Model of Leadership in Formal Organizations: A Developmental Approach." In J. G. Hunt & L. L. Larson (Eds.) *Leadership Frontiers*, (Kent, Ohio: Comparative Administration Research Institute, 1975) and House & Mitchell, *op. cit.*

7. A. J. Melcher, *Structure and Process of Organizations: A Systems Approach*, (Englewood Cliffs, N. J.: Prentice-Hall, 1976); R. N. Osborn & J. G. Hunt, "Environment and Organizational Effectiveness," *Administrative Science Quarterly*, 1974, *19*, pp. 231-246.

8. D. S. Pugh, D. J. Hickson, C. R. Hinings & C. Turner, "Dimensions of Organization Structure," *Administrative Science Quarterly*, 1968, *13*, pp. 65-105 and J. C. Taylor, "Technology and Supervision in the Post-Industrial Era." In J. G. Hunt & L. L. Larson (Eds.) *Contingency Approaches to Leadership*, (Carbondale, Illinois: Southern Illinois University Press, 1974).

9. J. G. Hunt, R. N. Osborn & R. S. Schuler, "Relations of Discretionary and Nondiscretionary Leadership to Performance and Satisfaction in a Complex Organization," Unpublished paper, Department of Administrative Sciences, Southern Illinois University at Carbondale, 1976; and, R. N. Osborn & J. G. Hunt, "Environment and Leadership: Discretionary and Nondiscretionary Leader Behavior and Organizational Outcomes," Unpublished paper, Department of Business Administration, University of Texas at Arlington, Texas, 1977.

10. J. G. Hunt, R. N. Osborn & L. L. Larson, "Upper Level Technical Orientation and First-Level Leadership Within a Contingency and Contingency Framework," *Academy of Management Journal*, 1975, *18*, pp. 475-488. R. Likert, "An Evolving Concept of Human Resources Accounting," (Paper presented at the American Psychological Association meetings, 1973); R. E. Miles, *Theories of Management: Implications for Organizational Behavior and Development*, (New York, McGraw-Hill, 1975); and J. C. Taylor, *op. cit.*

11. Taylor, *op. cit.*

12. Melcher, *op. cit.*

13. Melcher, *op. cit.*; and Pugh et al., *op. cit.*

14. T. Burns & G. M. Stalker, *The Management of Innovation*, (London: Tavistock Publishing, 1961).

15. Burns & Stalker, *op. cit.*; and R. N. Osborn, J. G. Hunt & R. S. Bussom, "On Getting Your Own Way in Organizational Design: An Empirical Investigation of Requisite Variety," *Organization and Administrative Sciences*, in press.

16. J. Thompson, *Organizations in Action*, (New York: McGraw-Hill, 1967).

17. F. E. Fiedler, *A Theory of Leadership Effectiveness*, (New York: McGraw-Hill, 1967); House & Mitchell, *op. cit.* and Melcher, *op. cit.*

18. Kerr, *op. cit.*

19. J. G. Hunt, R. N. Osborn & C. A. Schriesheim, "Omissions and Commissions in Leadership Research," Unpublished paper, Department of Business Administration, University of Texas at Arlington, Texas, 1977; and, C. A. Schriesheim & S. Kerr, "Theories and Measures of Leadership: A Critical Appraisal of Current and Future Directions," in J. G.

Hunt & L. L. Larson (Eds.) *Leadership: The Cutting Edge*, (Carbondale, Illinois: Southern Illinois University Press, in press).

20. R. J. House & G. Dessler, "The Path-Goal Theory of Leadership: Some *Post Hoc* and *A Priori* Tests," In J. G. Hunt & L. L. Larson (Eds.) *Contingency Approaches to Leadership, op. cit.*

21. J. G. Hunt & R. N. Osborn, "Machiavellianism: The Manipulative Side of Leadership," Southwest Division, Academy of Management, *1976, Proceedings*, San Antonio, pp. 73-77.

22. We have considered both initiating structure and consideration to serve several functions. Sometimes, as in House and Mitchell, (this volume), one will see some of these functions served by additional leadership dimensions.

23. L. W. Porter, "Organizational Politics," Address delivered at the Southwest Division, Academy of Management meetings, New Orleans, 1976. (See R. J. Hills, "The Representative Function: Neglected Dimension of Leadership Behavior," *Administrative Science Quarterly*, 1963, *8*, pp. 83-101; R. N. Osborn & J. G. Hunt, "An Empirical Investigation of Lateral and Vertical Leadership at Two Organizational Levels," *Journal of Business Research*, 1974, *2*, pp. 209-221. (a) R. N. Osborn & J. G. Hunt, "Environment and Organizational Effectiveness," *Administrative Science Quarterly*, 1974, *19*, pp. 231-246, and (b), L. R. Sayles, *Managerial Behavior*, (New York: McGraw-Hill, 1964).

24. M. Puzo, *The Godfather*, (Greenwich, Connecticut: Fawcett, 1969).

25. A. Gouldner, "The Norm of Reciprocity: A Preliminary Statement," *American Sociological Review*, 1960, *25*, pp. 161-178.

26. J. B. Rotter, "Generalized Expectancies for Internal Versus External Control of Reinforcement," *Psychological Monographs*, 1966, *80*, pp. 1-28.

27. J. G. Miner, *The Challenge of Managing*, (Philadelphia: Saunders, 1975).

28. J. P. Campbell, M. D. Dunnette, E. E. Lawler & K. E. Weick, *Managerial Behavior, Performance and Effectiveness*, (New York: McGraw-Hill, 1970) and, J. G. Hunt, "Another Look at Human Relations Training," *Training and Development Journal*, 1968, *22*, pp. 2-10.

29. F. E. Fiedler & M. M. Chemers, *Leadership and Effective Management*, (New York: Scott Foresman, 1974).

Chapter 5

DECISION MAKING AND THE LEADERSHIP PROCESS*

Victor H. Vroom

This article deals with the intersection of two areas of scientific inquiry and with the results of an extensive program of research to explore that intersection. The first area is the process of decision making. Recent developments in the theory of decision making suggest the usefulness of focussing on the processes by which decisions are made by individuals, groups and organizations.[1] Instead of treating the social system as a "black box," researchers underscore the necessity of identifying the processes which intervene between problem and solution—the processes which ultimately control the decisions that are made.

The second area of inquiry is the study of leadership. From early searches for universal leadership traits and from more recent efforts to uncover patterns of leader behavior which are consistently related to group effectiveness has come widespread support for situational or contingency leadership. Such questions as "Who would be the best leader?" or "How should a leader behave so as to stimulate the greatest productivity?" cannot be answered without a detailed knowledge of the contexts of the questions.[2]

To put these two developments together, one can conceive of the leader's role, at least in part, as controlling the processes by which decisions are made in that part of the organization for which he or she is responsible. The

* Reprinted with permission from The *Journal of Contemporary Business*, Autumn, 1974.

processes vary in a number of respects, but the one of most immediate interest and relevance to the study of leadership is the extent to which the leader encourages the participation of his or her subordinates in the decision-making process.

A manager who has five subordinates reporting to him illustrates this connection between leadership and decision making. Each subordinate has a clearly defined and distinct set of responsibilities. When one of them resigns to take a position with another organization because of a recent cost-cutting program which makes it impossible to hire new employees, the manager cannot replace this subordinate with someone else. It will be necessary to reallocate the departing subordinate's responsibilities among the remaining four to maintain the present workload and effectiveness of the unit.

This situation represents many circumstances faced by persons in leadership positions. There is some need for action—a problem exists and a solution, or decision, must be found. The leader has some areas of freedom or discretion (there are a number of possible ways in which the work can be reallocated), but there are also some constraints on his actions. For example, he cannot solve the problem by hiring someone from outside the organization. Furthermore, the solution is going to have effects on people other than himself; the subordinates must implement whatever decision is reached.

In this situation, a number of possible decision-making processes could be employed. The leader could make the decision by himself and announce it to his subordinates; he could obtain additional information from his subordinates and then make the decision; he could consult his subordinates, individually or collectively, before making the decision; or he could convene them as a group, share the problem and attempt to reach an agreement on the solution. These alternatives vary in terms of social, not cognitive, processes—specifically, the amount and type of opportunity afforded subordinates to participate in the decision.

Two theoretically distinct sets of questions can be asked concerning the leader's choice of a decision process. One contains the normative questions about which process should be used to make the decision. The other set consists of descriptive questions concerning which decision-making process actually would be used. This article describes the results of a research program aimed at answering these sets of questions.

Toward a Normative Model

What would be a rational way of deciding the form and amount of participation in decision-making appropriate in different situations? One can agree with the basic tenet of contingency theories that "leadership must depend upon the situation" but despair over the vacuous nature of this statement when faced with the task of specifying the kinds of situations which call for different approaches.

Clearly, one wants to select a decision process in a given situation that has the greatest likelihood of resulting in effective decisions, but the concept of effectiveness is far too general to be of much use for analytical purposes. There are at least three classes of outcomes that bear on the ultimate effectiveness of decisions:

- The quality or rationality of the decision,
- The acceptance or commitment on the part of subordinates to execute the decision effectively, and
- The amount of time required to make the decision.

Research dealing with the effects of the degree of subordinate participation in decision making on each of these outcomes concluded: "The results suggest that allocating problem-solving and decision-making tasks to entire groups requires a greater investment of manhours but produces higher acceptance of decisions and a higher probability that the decision will be executed efficiently. Differences between these two methods in quality of decisions and in elapsed time are inconclusive and probably highly variable. . . . It would be naive to think that group decision-making is always more "effective" than autocratic decision-making, or vice versa; the relative effectiveness of these two extreme methods depends both on the weights attached to quality, acceptance and time variables and on differences in amounts of these outcomes resulting from these methods, neither of which is invariant from one situation to another. The critics and proponents of participative management would do well to direct their efforts toward identifying the properties of situations in which different decision-making approaches are effective rather than wholesale condemnation or deification of one approach."[3]

Vroom and Yetton described a taxonomy of decision processes that is used throughout this article. The taxonomy is shown in Table 1. Each process is represented by a symbol, *e.g.*, AI, CI, GII; the first letter signifies the basic properties of the process (A stands for autocratic, C for consultative and G for group) and the Roman numerals constitute variants on that process. Thus, AI represents the first variant on an autocratic process and AII represents the second variant, etc.

The next step is to identify, in a manner consistent with available research evidence, properties of the situation that can be used in a model. In the model to be described, the situational attributes are characteristics of the problem to be solved or decision to be made rather than of the more

TABLE 1

TYPES OF MANAGEMENT-DECISION STYLES

AI	You solve the problem or make the decision yourself, using information available to you at that time.
AII	You obtain the necessary information from your subordinate(s), then decide on the solution to the problem yourself. You may or may not tell your subordinates what the problem is in getting the information from them. The role played by your subordinates in making the decision is clearly one of providing the necessary information to you, rather than generating or evaluating alternative solutions.
CI	You share the problem with relevant subordinates individually, getting their ideas and suggestions without bringing them together as a group. Then you make the decision that may or may not reflect your subordinates' influence.
CII	You share the problem with your subordinates as a group collectively, obtaining their ideas and suggestions. Then you make the decision that may or may not reflect your subordinates' influence.
GII*	You share a problem with your subordinates as a group. Together you generate and evaluate alternatives and attempt to reach agreement (consensus) on a solution. Your role is much like that of chairman. You do not try to influence the group to adopt "your" solution and you are willing to accept and implement any solution that has the support of the entire group.

*(GI is omitted because it applies only to more comprehensive models outside the scope of this article.)

general properties of the role of the leader. Table 2 shows the problem attributes in the present form of the model. For each attribute a question is provided that can be used by leaders in diagnosing problems. The terms used in Table 2 and the empirical basis for their inclusion in the model are described more completely in a more recent book by Vroom and Yetton.[4]

It has been found that trained managers can diagnose a particular problem quickly and quite reliably by answering this set of seven relevant questions. But how can such responses generate a prediction concerning the most effective decision process to be employed by the leader? What kind of normative model of leadership style can be constructed using this set of problem attributes?

Figure I shows one such model expressed in the form of a decision tree, the seventh version of such a model that we have developed over the last

TABLE 2
PROBLEM ATTRIBUTES USED IN THE MODEL

	Problem Attributes	Diagnostic Questions
A.	The importance of the quality of the decision.	Is there a quality requirement such that one solution is likely to be more rational than another?
B.	The extent to which the leader possesses sufficient information/expertise to make a high-quality decision by himself or herself.	Do I have sufficient information to make a high-quality decision?
C.	The extent to which the problem is structured.	Is the problem structured?
D.	The extent to which acceptance or commitment on the part of subordinates is critical to the effective implementation of the decision.	Is acceptance of the decision by subordinates critical to effective implementation?
E.	The prior probability that the leader's autocratic decision will receive acceptance by subordinates.	If I were to make the decision by myself, is it reasonably certain that it would be accepted by my subordinates?
F.	The extent to which subordinates are motivated to attain the organizational goals as represented in the objectives explicit in the statement of the problem.	Do subordinates share the organizational goals to be obtained in solving the problem?
G.	The extent to which subordinates are likely to be in conflict over preferred solutions.	Is conflict among subordinates likely in preferred solutions?

three years. The problem attributes, expressed in question form, are arranged along the top of the figure. To use the model for a particular decision-making situation, one starts at the left-hand side and works toward the right asking oneself the question immediately above any box encountered. When a terminal node is reached, a number will be found designating the problem type and one of the decision-making processes appearing in Table 1. AI is prescribed for four problem types (1, 2, 4 and 5); AII is prescribed for two problem types (9 and 10); CI is prescribed for only one problem type (8); CII is prescribed for four problem types (7, 11, 13 and

14); and GII is prescribed for three problem types (3, 6 and 12). The relative frequency with which each of the five decision processes would be prescribed for any manager would, of course, depend on the distribution of problem types encountered in his decision-making.

Figure 1
DECISION MODEL

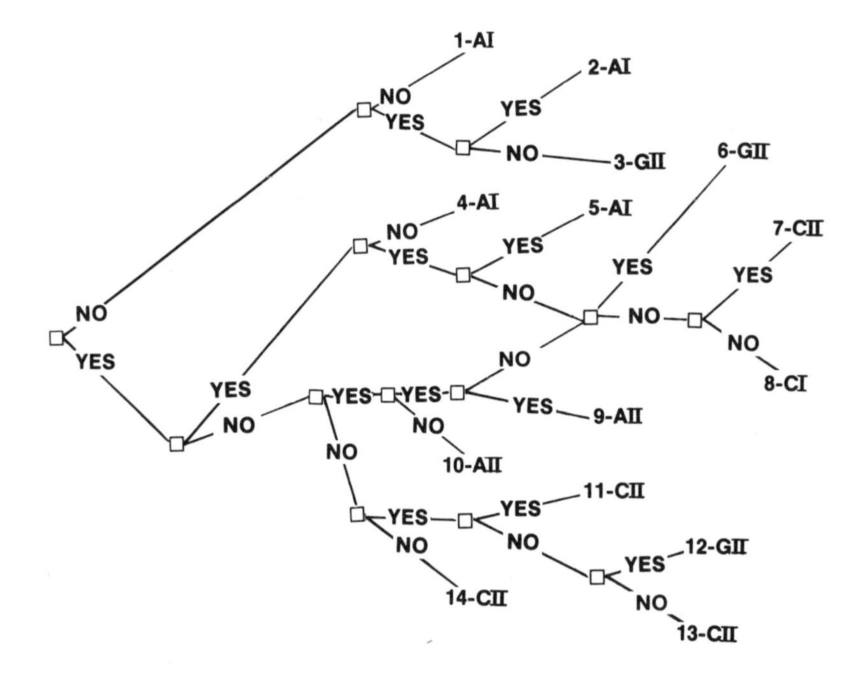

Rationale Underlying the Model

The decision processes specified for each problem type are not arbitrary. The model's behavior is governed by a set of principles intended to be consistent with evidence of the consequences of participation in decision-making on organizational effectiveness.

Two mechanisms underlie the behavior of the model. The first is a set of seven rules that protect the quality and acceptance of the decision by eliminating alternatives that risk one or the other of these decision outcomes. The second mechanism is a principle for choosing among alternatives in the feasible set where more than one exists.

The rules are examined first because they do much of the work of the model. As previously indicated, they intend to protect both the quality and acceptance of the decision.

In the form of the model shown, three rules protect decision quality.

- The Information Rule. If the quality of the decision is important and if the leader does not possess enough information or expertise to solve the problem by himself or herself, AI is eliminated from the feasible set. (Its use risks a low-quality decision.)
- The Goal-Congruence Rule. If the quality of the decision is important and if the subordinates do not share the organizational goals to be obtained in solving the problem, GII is eliminated from the feasible set. (Alternatives that eliminate the leader's final control over the decision reached may jeopardize the quality of the decision.)
- The Unstructured-Problem Rule. In decisions in which the quality of the decision is important, if the leader lacks the necessary information or expertise to solve the problem alone, and if the problem is unstructured, *i.e.*, he or she does not know exactly what information is needed and where it is located, the method used must provide not only for collection of information but also for collection in an efficient and effective manner. Methods that involve interaction among all subordinates with full knowledge of the problem are likely to be both more efficient and to generate a high-quality solution. Under these conditions, AI, AII and CI are eliminated from the feasible set. (AI does not allow the leader to collect the necessary information, and AII and CI represent more cumbersome, less effective and less efficient means of bringing the necessary information to bear on the solution of the problem than methods that permit persons with the necessary information to interact.)

In addition to the decision-quality rules, there are four rules to protect acceptance.

- The Acceptance Rule. If the acceptance of the decision by subordinates is critical to effective implementation, and if it is not certain that an autocratic decision made by the leader would receive that acceptance, AI and AII are eliminated from the feasible set. (Neither provides an opportunity for subordinates to participate in the decision and both risk the necessary acceptance.)

• The Conflict Rule. If the acceptance of the decision is critical, if an autocratic decision is not certain to be accepted, and if subordinates are likely to be in conflict or disagreement over the appropriate solution, AI, AII, and CI are eliminated from the feasible set. (The method used in solving the problem should enable those disagreeing to resolve their differences, with full knowledge of the problem. Accordingly, under these conditions, AI, AII, and CI—which involve no interaction or only "one-on-one" relationships and, therefore, provide no opportunity for those in conflict to resolve their differences—are eliminated from the feasible set. Their use runs the risk of leaving some subordinates with less than the necessary commitment to the final decision.)

• The Fairness Rule. If the quality of decision is unimportant and if acceptance is critical and not certain to result from an autocratic decision, AI, AII, CI and CII are eliminated from the feasible set. (The method used should maximize the probability of acceptance, for acceptance is the only relevant consideration in determining the effectiveness of the decision. Under these circumstances, AI, AII, CI and CII, which create less acceptance or commitment than GII, are eliminated from the feasible set. To use them is to run the risk of getting less than the needed acceptance of the decision.)

• The Acceptance Priority Rule. If acceptance is critical and is not assured by an autocratic decision, and if subordinates can be trusted, AI, AII, CI and CII are eliminated from the feasible set. (Methods that provide greater partnership in the decision-making process can provide greater acceptance without risking decision quality. Use of any method other than GII results in an unnecessary risk that the decision will not be fully accepted or receive the necessary commitment from subordinates.)

After these seven rules have been applied to a given problem, a feasible set of decision processes is generated (see Table 3). Clearly, there are some problem types for which only one method remains in the feasible set and others for which five methods remain feasible.

When more than one method remains in the feasible set, there are a number of ways to choose among them. In Figure I, the mechanism underlying choices utilizes the number of manhours used in solving the problem. Given a set of methods with equal likelihood of meeting both quality and acceptance requirements for the decision, the model indicates the method that requires the least investment in manhours. On the basis of the empirical evidence summarized earlier, this is the method furthest to the left within the feasible set. For example, because AI, AII, CI, CII and GII are all feasible as in Problem Types 1 and 2, AI would be the method chosen.

TABLE 3
PROBLEM TYPES AND THE FEASIBLE SET OF DECISION PROCESSES

Problem Type	Acceptable Methods
1	AI, AII, CI, CII, GII
2	AI, AII, CI, CII, GII
3	GII
4	AI, AII, CI, CII, GII*
5	AI, AII, CI, CII, GII*
6	GII
7	CII
8	CI, CII
9	AII, CI, CII, GII*
10	AII, CI, CII, GII*
11	CII, GII*
12	GII
13	CII
14	CII, GII*

* Within the feasible set only when the answer to question F is Yes.

The model is designed to protect the quality of the decision and to insure the expenditure of the least number of manhours in the process. Because it focuses on conditions surrounding making and implementing a particular decision rather than on any long-term considerations, it can be termed a short-term model.

However, it seems likely that leadership methods that may be optimal for short-term results may be different from those that would be optimal over a longer period of time. The manager who uses more participative methods could, in time, develop his or her subordinates, increasing not only the knowledge and talent that they could bring to bear on decisions but also their identification with the organization goals. A promising approach to development of a long-term model is one that places less weight on manhours as the basis for choice of method within the feasible set. Given a long-term orientation, one would be interested in the possibility of a tradeoff between manhours in problem solving and team development, both of which increase with participation. Viewed in these terms, the time-minimizing model places maximum relative weight on manhours and no weight on development; hence, it indicates the style furthest to the left within the feasible set. If these assumptions are correct, a model that places less weight on manhours and more weight on development would dictate a style further to the right within the feasible set.

The model just described is the latest of a set of such models which have been devised over the last few years. Undoubtedly, it is not perfect and will be amended or altered as additional research evidence becomes available.

It should be noted that the domain of decisions to which this model has been addressed are what Maier, Solem and Maier refer to as "group problems," *i.e.*, decisions which affect all or a major subset of the subordinates reporting to the leader.[5] However, a substantial number of problems confronting the leader may affect only one of his (her) subordinates. These "individual problems" fall outside the domain of the model described here, but a similar model has been developed to deal with them. This model utilizes additional decision processes, including delegation of the decision to the affected subordinate.[6] Substantial similarity between the problem attributes used for group and individual problems has made it possible to present the models in a single decision tree.

Toward a Descriptive Model

In addition to the development of normative or prescriptive models, research also has been directed toward how leaders do, in fact, behave when confronted with problems to solve or decisions to make. What considerations affect the decision processes they employ? What factors both within their personal makeup and in the situations they face cause leaders to retain or share their decision-making power with their subordinates? In what respects is their behavior similar to our different-from-the-normative model?

Two different research methods have been used in an attempt to answer such questions. The first investigation utilized a method that can be referred to as "recalled problems." Over 500 managers from 11 different countries and from a variety of firms were asked to provide a written description of a problem that they had recently had to solve. The problems varied in length from one paragraph to several pages and covered virtually every facet of managerial decision making. Each manager was asked to indicate which of the decision processes shown in Table 1 was used to solve the problem. Finally, each manager was asked to answer the questions shown in Table 2 corresponding to the problem attributes used in the normative model.

These data made it possible to determine the frequency with which the managers' decision process was similar to that of the normative model. It also illustrated the factors in their description of the situation which were associated with the use of each decision process. This investigation provided interesting results but, more importantly, it provided the basis for a second more powerful method for investigating the same questions. This second method, "standardized problems," used the actual cases written by the managers in the construction of a standardized set of cases, each of which depicts a manager faced with a problem to solve or decision to make. In each case, a leader is asked to assume the role of the manager faced with the situation described and to indicate which decision process he or she would use if faced with that situation.

Several such sets of cases have been developed. In early research, each set consisted of 30 cases corresponding to the definition of group problems. Recently a set of 48 cases, one-half group problems and one-half individual problems, has been used for research purposes.[7]

Composition of each set of standardized cases was in accordance with multifactorial experimental design. The seven problem attributes used in the normative model varied in each case, and variation in each attribute was independent of other attributes, allowing assessment of the effects of each problem attribute on the decision processes used by a given manager.

The cases spanned a wide range of managerial problems, including production scheduling, quality control, portfolio management, personnel allocation and R & D project selection. To date, several thousand managers in the United States and abroad have been studied.

It is not possible to summarize everything learned in the course of this research within the limits of this article, but some of the highlights are presented. Since the results obtained from the two research methods—recalled and standardized problems—are consistent, the major results can be presented independently of the method used.

Major Results

Perhaps most striking is the finding that weakens the widespread view that participativeness is a general trait that individual managers exhibit in different amounts. To be sure, there were differences among managers in their general tendencies to utilize participative methods as opposed to autocratic ones. On the standardized problems, these differences accounted for about 10 percent of the total variance in the decision processes. Furthermore, managers who tended to use more participative methods, such as CII and GII, with group problems also tended to use more participative methods, like delegation, for dealing with individual problems.

However, these differences in behavior among managers were small in comparison with differences within managers. On the standardized problems, no manager indicated that he or she would use the same decision process on all problems or decisions, and most managers use all methods in some circumstances.

Some of this variance in behavior within managers can be attributed to widely shared tendencies to respond to some situations by sharing power and to other situations by retaining it. It makes more sense to talk about participative and autocratic managers. In fact, on the standardized group problems, the variance in behavior across problems or cases is about three times as large as the variance across managers, and, on standardized individual problems, situational variance exceeds variance among people by a factor of five.

What are the characteristics of a situation which elicits autocratic rather than participative leadership? The answer constitutes a partial descriptive model of this aspect of the decision-making process and has been the goal of much of the research conducted. From observations of behavior on both recalled and standardized problems, it is clear that the decision-making process employed by a typical manager is influenced by a large number of factors, many of which also show up in the normative model. Several conclusions substantiated by the results on both recalled and standardized problems are that: Managers use decision processes providing less opportunity for participation (1) when they possess all the necessary information, (2) when the problem they face is well-structured rather than unstructured, (3) when their subordinates' acceptance of the decision is not critical for the effective implementation of the decision or when the prior probability of acceptance of an autocratic decision is high, and (4) when the personal goals of their subordinates are not congruent with the goals of the organization as manifested in the problem.

These findings concern relatively common or widely shared ways of dealing with organizational problems. Other results suggest that managers have different ways of "tailoring" their decision process to the situation. Theoretically, these can be thought of as differences among managers in decision rules about when to encourage participation. Statistically, the differences are represented as interactions between situational variables and personal characteristics.

For example, consider two managers who have identical distributions of the use of the five decision processes shown in Table 1 on a set of 30 cases. In a sense, they are equally participative (or autocratic); however, the situations in which they permit or encourage participation in decision making on the part of their subordinates may be very different. One may restrict the participation of subordinates to decisions without a quality requirement while the other may restrict their participation to problems with a quality requirement. The former would be more inclined to use participative-decision processes (like GII) on decisions such as what color the walls should be painted or when the company picnic should be held. The latter would be more likely to encourage participation in making decisions that have a clear and demonstrable impact on the organization's success in achieving its external goals.

Use of the standardized problem set permits the assessment of such differences in decision rules that govern choices among decision-making processes. Because the cases are selected in accordance with an experimental design, they can indicate differences in the behavior of managers attributable not only to the existence of a quality requirement in the problem but also to the effects of acceptance requirements, conflict, information requirements, etc.

Behavior of the Model vs. Manager Behavior

The research using recalled and standardized problems has also permitted examination of similarities and differences between the behavior of the normative model and the behavior of a typical manager. This analysis reveals, at the very least, what behavioral changes can be expected if managers begin using the normative model as the basis for choosing their decision-making processes.

A typical manager says he or she would (or did) use the same decision process as that in Figure 1 in about 40 percent of group problems. In two-thirds of the situations, his or her behavior is consistent with the feasible set of methods proposed in the model. However, in the remaining one-third of the situations, the behavior violates at least one of the seven rules underlying the model. Results show significantly higher agreement with the normative model for individual problems than for group problems.

The four rules designed to protect the acceptance of or commitment to the decision have substantially higher probabilities of being violated than the three rules designed to protect the quality or rationality of the decision. One of the acceptance rules, the Fairness Rule (Rule 6), is violated almost 75 percent of the time that it could have been violated. On the other hand, one of the quality rules, the Information Rule (Rule 1), is violated in only about 3 percent of the occasions in which it is applicable. If we assume for the moment that these two sets of rules have equal validity, the findings strongly suggest that the decisions made by typical managers are more likely to prove ineffective because of deficiencies of acceptance by subordinates rather than because of deficiencies in decision quality.

Another striking difference between the behavior of the model and that of the typical manager is that model behavior shows far greater variance with the situation. If a typical manager voluntarily used the model as the basis for choosing his or her methods of making decisions, this manager would become both more autocratic and more participative. He or she would employ autocratic methods more frequently in situations in which subordinates were unaffected by the decision. Also, this manager would use participative methods more frequently when his or her subordinates' cooperation and support were critical and/or their information and expertise were required.

It should be noted that the typical manager to whom we refer is merely a statistical average of the several thousand who have been studied over the last three or four years; thus, there is a great deal of variation around that average. As evidenced by their behavior on standardized problems, some managers already behave in a manner that is highly consistent with the model, while others' behavior is clearly at variance with it.

Implications for Leadership Training

The research program just summarized was conducted to shed new light on the causes and consequences of decision-making processes used by leaders in formal organizations. The course of the research shows that the data collection procedures, with appropriate additions and modifications, might also serve a useful function in leadership development. From this realization evolved a new approach to leadership training based on the concepts in the normative model and the empirical methods of the descriptive research.

A detailed description of this training program and of initial attempts to evaluate its effectiveness is based on the premise that one critical skill required of all leaders is the ability to adapt their behavior to the demands of the situation and that a component of this skill involves selecting the appropriate decision-making process for each problem or decision he or she confronts. The purpose of the program is not to "train" managers to use the model in their everyday decision-making activities. Instead, the model serves as a device for encouraging managers to examine their leadership styles and to come to a conscious realization of their own, often implicit, choices among decision processes, including their similarity and dissimilarity with the model. By helping managers to become aware of their present behavior and of alternatives to it, the training provides a basis for rethinking leadership styles, and making them more consistent with goals and objectives. Succinctly, the training is intended to transform habits into choices rather than to program a leader with a particular method of making choices.

A fundamental part of the program in its present form is the use of the set of standardized cases described earlier. Each participant specifies the decision process to be employed if he or she were the leader described in the case. Responses to the entire set of cases (usually 30 or 48) are processed by the computer, which generates a highly detailed analysis of the leadership style. The responses for all participants in a single course typically are processed simultaneously, permitting the calculation of differences among persons in the same program.

In its present form, a single computer printout for a person consists of three 15″ x 11″ pages, each filled with graphs and tables highlighting different features of behavior. Understanding the results requires a knowledge of the concepts underlying the model, an awareness already developed in one of the previous phases of the training program. The printout is accompanied by a manual that explains the results and provides suggested steps to follow to extract full meaning from the printout.

A few of the questions that the printout answers are:

- How autocratic or participative am I in my dealings with subordinates in comparison with other participants in the program?
- What decision processes do I use more or less frequently than the average?
- How close does my behavior come to that of the model? How frequently does my behavior agree with the feasible set? What evidence is there that my leadership style reflects the pressure of time as opposed to a concern with the development of my subordinates? How do I compare in these respects with other participants in the class?
- What rules do I violate most frequently and least frequently? On what cases did I violate these rules? Does my leadership style reflect more concern with getting decisions that are high in quality or with getting decisions that are accepted?

When a typical manager receives the printout, he or she immediately tries to understand what it reveals. After most of the major results are understood, this manager goes back to the set of cases to reread those in which he or she has violated rules. Typically, managers show an interest in discussing and comparing their results with others in the program, so groups of four to six persons gather to do this—a process which has been included as part of the program.

It should be emphasizesd that this method of providing feedback on leadership style is just one part of the total training experience which encompasses more than 30 hours over three successive days. To date, no long-term evaluations of its effectiveness have been undertaken but initial results appear quite promising.

Summary

This article provides a brief overview of some of the principal results of a research program aimed at increasing understanding of certain facets of the leadership process, most notably the role of the leader in the decision-making process. Two goals guide the inquiry; the first is normative and concerns the role that leaders should play in the process of making decisions. The second goal is descriptive and involves the role that leaders do play in the decision-making process. The normative model presented, one form of contingency model, stresses that leaders should adapt their role in the decision-making process to the demands of the situation. Further, results show that leaders do attempt to adapt their behavior to the situation, although in ways that are not perfectly consistent with the normative model. Finally, there is a description of a leadership training program which utilizes the concepts of the normative model and some empirical research methods to develop more effective leadership in organizations.

NOTES

* The research on which this paper is based was sponsored by the Organizational Effectiveness Research Programs, Psychological Sciences Division Office of Naval Research. (Control No. NOO 14-67-A-0097-0027, Control Authority Identification NO. NR-177-935).

1. J. G. March and H. A. Simon, *Organizations* (New York: Wiley, 1958); R. M. Cyert and J. G. March, *A Behavioral Theory of the Firm* (Englewood Cliffs, N.J.: Prentice-Hall, 1963); A. Newell and H. A. Simon, *Human Problem Solving* (New York: Prentice Hall, 1972).

2. F. E. Fiedler, *A Theory of Leadership Effectiveness* (New York: McGraw Hill, 1967); V. H. Vroom, "Leadership," M. Dunnette, ed. *Handbook of Industrial and Organizational Psychology* (Chicago: Rand McNally, 1974, in press).

3. V. H. Vroom, "Industrial Social Psychology," in G. Lindzey and E. Aronson, eds., *Handbook of Social Psychology*, Vol. 5 (Reading, Mass.: Addison-Wesley, 1970), pp. 239-240.

4. V. H. Vroom and G. W. Yetton, *Leadership and Decision-Making* (Pittsburgh: University of Pittsburgh Press, 1973).

5. N. R. F. Maier, A. R. Solem and A. A. Maier, *Supervisory and Executive Development: A Manual for Role Playing* (New York: Wiley, 1957).

6. V. H. Vroom and A. G. Jago, "Decision-Making As a Social Process: Normative and Descriptive Models of Leader Behavior," *Decision Sciences*, Vol. 5 (1974), pp. 743-769.

7. *Ibid.*

Part 3

LEADER, FOLLOWER, AND TASK

Chapter 6

PATH-GOAL THEORY OF LEADERSHIP*

Robert J. House

Terence R. Mitchell

An integrated body of conjecture by students of leadership, referred to as the "Path-Goal Theory of Leadership," is currently emerging. According to this theory, leaders are effective because of their impact on subordinates' motivation, ability to perform effectively and satisfactions. The theory is called path-goal because its major concern is how the leader influences the subordinates' perceptions of their work goals, personal goals and paths to goal attainment. The theory suggests that a leader's behavior is motivating or satisfying to the degree that the behavior increases subordinate goal attainment and clarifies the paths to these goals.

Historical Foundations

The path-goal approach has its roots in a more general motivational theory called expectancy theory.[1] Briefly, expectancy theory states that an individual's attitudes (*e.g.*, satisfaction with supervision or job satisfaction) or behavior (*e.g.*, leader behavior or job effort) can be predicted from: (1)

* Reprinted with permission from The *Journal of Contemporary Business*, Autumn, 1974.

the degree to which the job, or behavior, is seen as leading to various outcomes (expectancy) and (2) the evaluation of these outcomes (valences). Thus, people are satisfied with their job if they think it leads to things that are highly valued, and they work hard if they believe that effort leads to things that are highly valued. This type of theoretical rationale can be used to predict a variety of phenomena related to leadership, such as why leaders behave the way they do or how leader behavior influences subordinate motivation.[2]

This latter approach is the primary concern of this article. The implication for leadership is that subordinates are motivated by leader behavior to the extent that this behavior influences expectancies, *e.g.*, goal paths and valences, *e.g.*, goal attractiveness.

Several writers have advanced specific hypotheses concerning how the leader affects the paths and the goals of subordinates.[3] These writers focused on two issues: (1) how the leader affects subordinates' expectations that effort will lead to effective performance and valued rewards, and (2) how this expectation affects motivation to work hard and perform well.

While the state of theorizing about leadership in terms of subordinates' paths and goals is in its infancy, we believe it is promising for two reasons. First, it suggests effects of leader behavior that have not yet been investigated but which appear to be fruitful areas of inquiry. And, second, it suggests with some precision the situational factors on which the effects of leader behavior are contingent.

This initial theoretical work by Evans asserts that leaders will be effective by making rewards available to subordinates and by making these rewards contingent on the subordinate's accomplishment of specific goals.[4] Evans argued that one of the strategic functions of the leader is to clarify for subordinates the kind of behavior that leads to goal accomplishment and valued rewards. This function might be referred to as path clarification. Evans also argued that the leader increases the rewards available to subordinates by being supportive of subordinates, *i.e.*, by being concerned about their status, welfare and comfort. Leader supportiveness is in itself a reward that the leader has at his or her disposal, and the judicious use of this reward increases the motivation of subordinates.

Evans studied the relationship between the behavior of leaders and the subordinates' expectations that effort leads to rewards and also studied the resulting impact on ratings of the subordinates' performance. He found that when subordinates viewed leaders as being supportive (considerate of their needs) and when these superiors provided directions and guidance to the subordinates, there was a positive relationship between leader behavior and subordinates' performance ratings.

However, leader behavior was only related to subordinates' performance when the leader's behavior also was related to the subordinates' expectations that their effort would result in desired rewards. Thus, Evans' findings suggest that the major impact of a leader on the performance of subordinates is clarifying the path to desired rewards and making such rewards contingent on effective performance.

Stimulated by this line of reasoning, House, and House and Dessler advanced a more complex theory of the effects of leader behavior on the motivation of subordinates.[5] The theory explains the effects of four specific kinds of leader behavior on the following three subordinate attitudes or expectations: (1) the satisfaction of subordinates, (2) the subordinates' acceptance of the leader and (3) the expectations of subordinates that effort will result in effective performance and that effective performance is the path to rewards. The four kinds of leader behavior included in the theory are: (1) directive leadership, (2) supportive leadership, (3) participative leadership and (4) achievement-oriented leadership. Directive leadership is characterized by a leader who lets subordinates know what is expected of them, gives specific guidance as to what should be done and how it should be done, makes his or her part in the group understood, schedules work to be done, maintains definite standards of performance and asks that group members follow standard rules and regulations. Supportive leadership is characterized by a friendly and approachable leader who shows concern for the status, well-being and needs of subordinates. Such a leader does little things to make the work more pleasant, treats members as equals and is friendly and approachable. Participative leadership is characterized by a leader who consults with subordinates, solicits their suggestions and takes these suggestions seriously into consideration before making a decision. An achievement-oriented leader sets challenging goals, expects subordinates to perform at their highest level, continuously seeks improvement in performance and shows a high degree of confidence that the subordinates will assume responsibility, put forth effort and accomplish challenging goals. This kind of leader constantly emphasizes excellence in performance and simultaneously displays confidence that subordinates will meet high standards of excellence.

A number of studies suggest that these different leadership styles can be shown by the same leader in various situations.[6] For example, a leader may show directiveness toward subordinates in some instances and be participative or supportive in other instances.[7] Thus, the traditional method of characterizing a leader as either highly participative and supportive or highly directive is invalid; rather, it can be concluded that leaders vary in the particular fashion employed for supervising their subordinates. Also, the path-goal theory, in its present stage, is a tentative explanation of the effects of leader behavior—it is incomplete because it does not explain other kinds of leader behavior and does not explain the effects of the leader on factors other than subordinate acceptance, satisfaction and expectations. However, the theory is stated so that additional variables may be included in it as new knowledge is made available.

Path-Goal Theory

General Propositions

The first proposition of path-goal theory is that leader behavior is acceptable and satisfying to subordinates to the extent that the subordinates see such behavior as either an immediate source of satisfaction or as instrumental to future satisfaction.

The second proposition of this theory is that the leader's behavior will be motivational, *i.e.*, increase effort, to the extent that (1) such behavior makes satisfaction of subordinate's needs contingent on effective performance and (2) such behavior complements the environment of subordinates by providing the coaching, guidance, support and rewards necessary for effective performance.

These two propositions suggest that the leader's strategic functions are to enhance subordinates' motivation to perform and to increase satisfaction with the job and acceptance of the leader. From previous research on expectancy theory of motivation, it can be inferred that the strategic functions of the leader consist of: (1) recognizing and/or arousing subordinates' needs for outcomes over which the leader has some control, (2) increasing personal payoffs to subordinates for work-goal attainment, (3) making the path to those payoffs easier to travel by coaching and direction, (4) helping subordinates clarify expectancies, (5) reducing frustrating barriers and (6) increasing the opportunities for personal satisfaction, contingent on effective performance.

Stated less formally, the motivational functions of the leader consist of increasing the number and kinds of personal payoffs to subordinates for work-goal attainment and of making paths to these payoffs easier to travel by clarifying the paths, reducing road blocks and pitfalls, and increasing the opportunities for personal satisfaction en route.

Contingency Factors

Two classes of situational variables are asserted to be contingency factors. A contingency factor is a variable which moderates the relationship between two other variables such as leader behavior and subordinate satisfaction. For example, we might suggest that the degree of structure in the task moderates the relationship between leaders' directive behaviors and subordinates' job satisfaction. Figure 1 shows how such a relationship might look. Thus, subordinates are satisfied with directive behavior in an unstructured task and are satisfied with nondirective behavior in a structured task. Therefore, we say that the relationship between leader directiveness and subordinate satisfaction is contingent upon the structure of the task.

Figure 1
Hypothetical Relationship Between Directive Leadership and Subordinate Satisfaction With Task Structure as a Contingency Factor

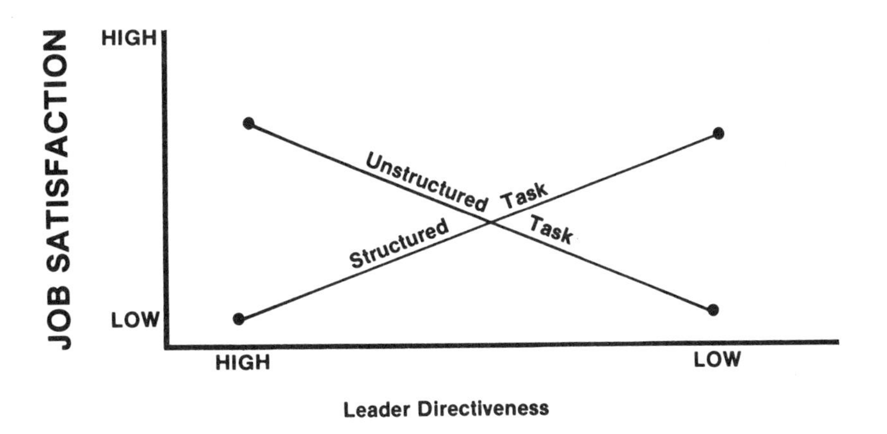

The two contingency variables are (a) personal characteristics of the subordinates and (b) the environmental pressures and demands with which subordinates must cope in order to accomplish the work goals and to satisfy their needs. While other situational factors also may operate to determine the effects of leader behavior, they are not presently known.

With respect to the first class of contingency factors, the characteristics of subordinates, path-goal theory asserts that leader behavior will be acceptable to subordinates to the extent that the subordinates see such behavior as either an immediate source of satisfaction or as instrumental to future satisfaction. Subordinates' characteristics are hypothesized to partially determine this perception. For example, Runyon[8] and Mitchell[9] show that the subordinate's score on a measure called Locus of Control moderates the relationship between participative leadership style and subordinate satisfaction. The Locus-of-Control measure reflects the degree to which an individual sees the environment as systematically responding to his or her behavior. People who believe that what happens to them occurs because of their behavior are called *internals*; people who believe that what happens to them occurs because of luck or chance are called *externals*. Mitchell's findings suggest that internals are more satisfied with a participative leadership style and that externals are more satisfied with a directive style.

A second characteristic of subordinates on which the effects of leader behavior are contingent is subordinates' perception of their own ability with respect to their assigned tasks. The higher the degree of perceived ability relative to task demands, the less the subordinate will view leader directiveness and coaching behavior as acceptable. Where the subordinate's perceived ability is high, directive behavior is likely to have little positive effect on the motivation of the subordinate and is likely to be perceived as excessively close control. Thus, the acceptability of the leader's behavior is determined in part by the characteristics of the subordinates.

The second aspect of the situation, the environment of the subordinate, consists of those factors that are not within the control of the subordinate but which are important to need satisfaction or to ability to perform effectively. The theory asserts that effects of the leader's behavior on the psychological states of subordinates are contingent on other parts of the subordinates' environment that are relevant to subordinate motivation. Three broad classifications of contingency factors in the environment are:

- The subordinates' tasks,
- The formal authority system of the organization, and
- The primary work group.

Assessment of the environmental conditions makes it possible to predict the kind and amount of influence that specific leader behaviors will have on the motivation of subordinates. Any of the three environmental factors could act upon the subordinate in any of three ways: first, to serve as stimuli that motivate and direct the subordinate to perform necessary task operations; second, to constrain variability in behavior (Constraints may help the subordinate by clarifying expectancies that effort leads to rewards or by preventing the subordinate from experiencing conflict and confusion. Constraints also may be counterproductive to the extent that they restrict initiative or prevent increases in effort from being associated positively with rewards.), and third, to serve as rewards for achieving desired performance; *e.g.*, it is possible for the subordinate to receive the necessary cues to do the job and the needed rewards for satisfaction from sources other than the leader, *e.g.*, co-workers in the primary work group. Thus, the impact of the leader on subordinates' motivation will be determined by the deficiency of the environment in motivational stimuli, constraints, or rewards.

With respect to the environment, path-goal theory asserts that when goals and paths to desired goals are apparent because of the routine nature of the task, clear group norms, or objective controls of the formal authority systems, attempts by the leader to clarify paths and goals will be both redundant and seen by subordinates as imposing unnecessary, close control. Although such control may increase performance by preventing "soldiering" or malingering, it also will result in decreased satisfaction (see Figure 1). Also with respect to the work environment, the theory asserts that the more dissatisfying the task, the more the subordinates will resent leader behavior directed at increasing productivity or enforcing compliance to organizational rules and procedures.

Finally, with respect to environmental variables, the theory states that leader behavior will be motivational to the extent that it helps subordinates cope with environmental uncertainties, threats from others or sources of frustration. Such leader behavior is predicted to increase subordinates' satisfaction with the job context and to be motivational to the extent that it increases the subordinates' expectations that their efforts will lead to valued rewards.

These propositions and specification of situational contingencies provide a heuristic framework on which to base future research, which, it is hoped, will lead to a more fully developed, explicitly formal theory of leadership.

Figure 2 presents a summary of the theory. Ideally these propositions, while admittedly tentative, will provide managers with some insights concerning the effects of their own leader behavior and that of others.

Empirical Support

The theory has been tested in a limited number of studies which have generated considerable empirical support for our ideas and which also suggest areas in which the theory requires revision. A brief review of these studies follows.

Leader Directiveness

Leader directiveness has a positive correlation with satisfaction and

Figure 2
SUMMARY OF PATH-GOAL RELATIONSHIPS

Leader Behavior	and	Contingency Factors	Cause	Subordinate Attitudes & Behavior
1 Directive 2 Supportive		1 Subordinate Characteristics Authoritarianism Locus of Control Influence Ability	Personal Perceptions	1 Job Satisfaction Job→Rewards 2 Acceptance of Leader Leader Rewards
3 Achievement-Oriented 4 Participative		2 Environmental Factors The Task Influence Formal Authority System Primary Work Group	Motivational Stimuli Constraints Rewards	3 Motivational Behavior Effort→Performance→ Performance→Rewards

expectancies of subordinates who are engaged in ambiguous tasks and has a negative correlation with satisfaction and expectancies of subordinates engaged in clear tasks. These findings were predicted by the theory and have been replicated in seven organizations. They suggest that when task demands are ambiguous or when the organization procedures, rules, and policies are not clear, a leader behaving in a directive manner complements the tasks and the organization by providing the necessary guidance and psychological structure for subordinates.[10] However, when task demands are clear to subordinates, leader directiveness is seen more as a hindrance.

However, other studies have failed to confirm these findings.[11] A study by Dessler[12] suggests a resolution to these conflicting findings. He found that for subordinates at the lower organizational levels of a manufacturing firm who were doing routine, repetitive, unambiguous tasks, directive leadership was preferred by closed-minded, dogmatic, authoritarian subordinates and nondirective leadership was preferred by non-authoritarian, open-minded subordinates. However, for subordinates at higher organizational levels doing nonroutine, ambiguous tasks, directive leadership was preferred by both authoritarian and nonauthoritarian subordinates. Thus, Dessler found that two contingency factors appear to operate simultaneously: subordinate task ambiguity and degree of subordinate authoritarianism. When measured in combination, the findings are as predicted by the theory; however, when the subordinate's personality is not taken into account, task ambiguity does not always operate as a contingency variable as predicted by the theory. House, Burrill and Dessler recently found a similar interaction between subordinate authoritarianism and task ambiguity in a second manufacturing firm, thus adding confidence in Dessler's original findings.[13]

Supportive Leadership

The theory hypothesizes that supportive leadership will have its most positive effect on subordinate satisfaction for subordinates who work on stressful, frustrating or dissatisfying tasks. This hypothesis has been tested in ten samples of employees,[14] and in only one of these studies was the hypothesis not confirmed.[15] Despite some inconsistency in research on supportive leadership, the evidence is sufficiently positive to suggest that managers should be alert to the critical need for supportive leadership under conditions where tasks are dissatisfying, frustrating or stressful to subordinates.

Achievement-Oriented Leadership

The theory hypothesizes that achievement-oriented leadership will cause subordinates to strive for higher standards of performance and to have more confidence in their ability to meet challenging goals. A recent study by House, Valency and Van der Krabben provides a partial test of this hypothesis among white collar employees in service organizations.[16] For subordinates performing ambiguous, nonrepetitive tasks, they found a positive relationship between the amount of achievement orientation of the leader and subordinates' expectancy that their effort would result in effective performance. Stated less technically, for subordinates performing ambiguous, nonrepetitive tasks, the higher the achievement orientation of the leader, the more the subordinates were confident that their efforts would pay off in effective performance. For subordinates performing moderately unambiguous, repetitive tasks, there was no significant relationship between achievement-oriented leadership and subordinate expectancies that their effort would lead to effective performance. This finding held in four separate organizations.

Two plausible interpretations may be used to explain these data. First, people who select ambiguous, nonrepetitive tasks may be different in personality from those who select a repetitive job and may, therefore, be more responsive to an achievement-oriented leader. A second explanation is that achievement orientation only affects expectancies in ambiguous situations because there is more flexibility and autonomy in such tasks. Therefore, subordinates in such tasks are more likely to be able to change in response to such leadership style. Neither of the above interpretations has been tested to date; however, additional research is currently under way to investigate these relationships.

Participative Leadership

In theorizing about the effects of participative leadership it is necessary to ask about the specific characteristics of both the subordinates and their situation that would cause participative leadership to be viewed as satisfying and instrumental to effective performance.

Mitchell recently described at least four ways in which a participative leadership style would impact on subordinate attitudes and behavior as predicted by expectancy theory.[17] First, a participative climate should increase the clarity of organizational contingencies. Through participation in decision making, subordinates should learn what leads to what. From a path-goal viewpoint participation would lead to greater clarity of the paths to various goals. A second impact of participation would be that subordinates should select goals they highly value. If one participates in decisions about various goals, it makes sense that this individual would select goals he or she wants. Thus, participation would increase the correspondence between organization and subordinate goals. Third, we can see how participation would increase the control the individual has over what happens on the job. If our motivation is higher (based on the preceding two points), then having greater autonomy and ability to carry out our intentions should lead to increased effort and performance. Finally, under a participative system, pressure towards high performance should come from sources other than the leader of the organization. More specifically, when people participate in the decision process they become more ego-involved; the decisions made are in some part their own. Also, their peers know what is expected and the social pressure has a greater impact. Thus, motivation to perform well stems from internal and social factors as well as from formal, external ones.

A number of investigations prior to the above formulation supported the idea that participation appears to be helpful,[18] and Mitchell presents a number of recent studies that support the above four points.[19] However, it is also true that we would expect the relationship between a participative style and subordinate behavior to be moderated by both the personality characteristics of the subordinate and the situational demands. Studies by Tannenbaum and Alport and Vroom have shown that subordinates who prefer autonomy and self-control respond more positively to participative leadership in terms of both satisfaction and performance than subordinates who do not have such preferences.[20] Also, the studies mentioned by Runyon[21] and Mitchell[22] showed that subordinates who were external in orientation were less satisfied with a participative style of leadership than were internal subordinates.

House also has reviewed these studies in an attempt to explain the ways in which the situation or environment moderates the relationship between participation and subordinate attitudes and behavior.[23] His analysis suggests that where participative leadership is positively related to satisfaction, regardless of the predispositions of subordinates, the tasks of the subjects appear to be ambiguous and ego-involving. In the studies in which the subjects' personalities or predispositions moderate the effect of participative leadership, the tasks of the subjects are inferred to be highly routine and/or non-ego-involving.

House reasoned from this analysis that the task may have an overriding effect on the relationship between leader participation and subordinate responses, and that individual predispositions or personality characteristics of subordinates may have an effect only under some tasks. It was assumed that when task demands are ambiguous, subordinates will have a need to reduce the ambiguity. Further, it was assumed that when task demands are ambiguous, participative problem solving between the leader and the subordinate will result in more effective decisions than when the task demands are unambiguous. Finally, it was assumed that when the subordinates are ego-involved in their tasks they are more likely to want to have a say in the decisions that affect them. Given these assumptions, the following hypotheses were formulated to account for the conflicting findings reviewed above:

- When subjects are highly ego-involved in a decision or a task and the decision or task demands are ambiguous, participative leadership will have a positive effect on the satisfaction and motivation of the subordinate, regardless of the subordinate's predisposition toward self-control, authoritarianism, or need for independence.
- When subordinates are not ego-involved in their tasks and when task demands are clear, subordinates who are not authoritarian and who have high needs for independence and self-control will respond favorably to leader participation and their opposite personality types will respond less favorably.

These hypotheses were derived on the basis of path-goal theorizing; *i.e.*, the rationale guiding the analysis of prior studies was that both task characteristics and characteristics of subordinates interact to determine the effect of a specific kind of leader behavior on the satisfaction, expectancies and performance of subordinates. To date, some of these predictions have been supported by one major investigation[24] in which personality variables, amount of participative leadership, task ambiguity, and job satisfaction were assessed for 324 employees of an industrial manufacturing organization. As expected, in nonrepetitive, ego-involving tasks, employees (regardless of their personality) were more satisfied under a participative style than a nonparticipative style. However, in repetitive tasks which were less ego-involving the amount of authoritarianism of subordinates moderated the relationship between leadership style and satisfaction. Specifically, low authoritarian subordinates were more satisfied under a participative style. These findings are exactly as the theory would predict; thus, it has promise in reconciling a set of confusing and contradictory findings with respect to participative leadership.

Summary and Conclusions

We have attempted to describe what we believe is a useful theoretical framework for understanding the effect of leadership behavior on subordinate satisfaction and motivation. Most theorists today have moved away from the simplistic notion that all effective leaders have a certain set of personality traits or that the situation completely determines performance. Some researchers have presented rather complex attempts at matching certain types of leaders with certain types of situations, *e.g.*, the articles written by Vroom and Fiedler in this issue. But we believe that a path-goal approach goes one step further. It not only suggests what type of style may be most effective in a given situation—it also attempts to explain why it is most effective.

We are optimistic about the future outlook of leadership research. With the guidance of path-goal theorizing, future research is expected to solve many confusing puzzles about the reasons for and effects of leader behavior that have not yet been solved. However, we add a word of caution: the theory, and the research on it, are relatively new to the literature of organizational behavior. Consequently, path-goal theory is offered more as a tool for directing research and stimulating insight than as a proven guide for managerial action.

NOTES

* This article is also to be reprinted in *Readings in Organizational and Industrial Psychology* by G. A. Yukl and K. N. Wexley, 2nd edition (1975). The research by House and his associates was partially supported by a grant from the Shell Oil Company of Canada. The research by Mitchell and his associates was partially supported by the Office of Naval Research Contract NR 170-761, N00014-67-A-0103-0032 (Terence R. Mitchell, Principal Investigator).

1. T. R. Mitchell, "Expectancy Model of Job Satisfaction, Occupational Preference and Effort: A Theoretical, Methodological and Empirical Appraisal," *Psychological Bulletin* (1974).

2. D. M. Nebeker and T. R. Mitchell, "Leader Behavior: An Expectancy Theory Approach," *Organizational Behavior and Human Performance*, 11 (1974), pp. 355-367.

3. M. G. Evans, "The Effects of Supervisory Behavior on the Path-Goal Relationship," *Organization Behavior and Human Performance*, 5 (1970), pp. 277-298; T. H. Hammer and H. T. Dachler, "The Process of Supervision in the Context of Motivation Theory," Research Report No. 3 (University of Maryland, 1973); F. Dansereau, Jr., J. Cashman and G. Graen, "Instrumentality Theory and Equity Theory As Complementary Approaches in Predicting the Relationship of Leadership and Turnover Among Managers," *Organization Behavior and Human Performances*, 10 (1973), pp. 184-200; R. J. House, "A Path-Goal Theory of Leader Effectiveness," *Administrative Science Quarterly*, 16, 3 (September 1971), pp. 321-338; T. R. Mitchell, "Motivation and Participation: An Integration," *Academy of Management Journal*, 16, 4 (1973), pp. 160-179; G. Graen, F. Dansereau, Jr. and T. Miniami, "Dysfunctional Leadership Styles," *Organization Behavior and Human Performance*, 7 (1972), pp. 216-236; and "An Empirical Test of the Man-in-the-Middle Hypothesis Among Executives in a Hierarchiacal Organization Employing a Unit Analysis," *Organization Behavior and Human Performance*, 8 (1972), pp. 262-285; R. J. House and G. Dessler, "The Path-Goal Theory of Leadership: Some Post Hoc and A Priori Tests," to appear in J. G. Hunt, ed., *Contingency Approaches to Leadership* (Carbondale, Ill.: Southern Illinois University Press, 1974).

4. M. G. Evans, "Effects of Supervisory Behavior", and "Extensions of a Path-Goal Theory of Motivation," *Journal of Applied Psychology*, 59 (1974), pp. 172-178.

5. House, "A Path-Goal Theory"; House and Dessler, "Path-Goal Theory of Leadership," *op. cit.*

6. R. J. House and G. Dessler, "Path-Goal Theory of Leadership"; R. M. Stogdill, *Managers, Employees, Organization* (Ohio State University, Bureau of Business Research, 1965); R. J. House, A. Valency and R. Van der Krabben, "Some Tests and Extensions of the Path-Goal Theory of Leadership" (in preparation).

7. W. A. Hill and D. Hughes, "Variations in Leader Behavior As a Function of Task Type," *Organization Behavior and Human Performance* (1974, in press).

8. K. E. Runyon, "Some Interactions Between Personality Variables and Management Styles," *Journal of Applied Psychology*, 57, 3 (1973), pp. 288-294; T. R. Mitchell, C. R. Smyser and S. E. Weed, "Locus of Control: Supervision and Work Satisfaction," *Academy of Management* (in press).

9. Mitchell *et al*, "Locus of Control."

10. R. J. House, "A Path-Goal Theory"; R. J. House and G. Dessler, "Path-Goal Theory of Leadership"; A. D. Szalagyi and H. P. Sims, "An Exploration of the Path-Goal Theory of Leadership in a Health Care Environment," *Academy of Management Journal* (in press); J. D. Dermer, "Supervisory Behavior and Budget Motivation" (Cambridge, Mass.: unpublished, MIT, Sloan School of Management, 1974); R. W. Smetana, "The Relationship Between Managerial Behavior and Subordinate Attitudes and Motivation: A Contribution to a Behavioral Theory of Leadership" (Ph.D. diss. Wayne State University, 1974).

11. S. E. Weed, T. R. Mitchell and C. R. Smyser, "A Test of House's Path-Goal Theory of Leadership in an Organizational Setting" (paper presented at Western Psychological Asso., 1974); J. D. Dermer and J. P. Siegel, "A Test of Path-Goal Theory: Disconfirming Evidence and a Critique" (unpublished, University of Toronto, Faculty of Management Studies, 1973); R. S. Schuler, "A Path-Goal Theory of Leadership: An Empirical Investigation" (Ph.D. diss., Michigan State University, 1973); H. K. Downey, J. E. Sheridan and J. W. Slocum, Jr., "Analysis of Relationships Among Leader Behavior, Subordinate Job Performance and Satisfaction: A Path-Goal Approach" (unpublished mimeograph, 1974); J. E. Stinson and T. W. Johnson, "The Path-Goal Theory of Leadership: A Partial Test and Suggested Refinement," *Proceedings* (Kent, Ohio: 7th Annual Conference of the Midwest Academy of Management, April 1974), pp. 18-36.

12. G. Dessler, "An Investigation of the Path-Goal Theory of Leadership" (Ph.D. diss., City University of New York, Bernard M. Baruch College, 1973).

13. R. J. House, D. Burrill and G. Dessler, "Tests and Extensions of Path-Goal Theory of Leadership, I" (unpublished, in process).

14. R. J. House, "A Path-Goal Theory"; ________ and G. Dessler, "Path-Goal Theory of Leadership"; A. D. Szalagyi and H. P. Sims, "Exploration of Path-Goal"; J. E. Stinson and T. W. Johnson, *Proceedings*; R. S. Schuler, "Path-Goal: Investigation"; H. K, Downey, J. E. Sheridan and J. W. Slocum, Jr., "Analysis of Relationships"; S. E. Weed, T. R. Mitchell and C. R. Smyser, "Test of House's Path-Goal."

15. A. D. Szalagyi and H. P. Sims, "Exploration of Path-Goal."

16. R. J. House, A. Valency and R. Van der Krabben, "Tests and Extensions of Path-Goal Theory of Leadership, II" (unpublished, in process).

17. T. R. Mitchell, "Motivation and Participation."

18. H. Tosi, "A Reexamination of Personality As a Determinant of the Effects of Participation," *Personnel Psychology*, 23 (1970), pp. 91-99; J. Sadler "Leadership Style, Confidence in Management and Job Satisfaction," *Journal of Applied Behavioral Sciences*, 6 (1970), pp. 3-19; K. N. Wexley, J. P. Singh and J. A. Yukl, "Subordinate Personality As a Moderator of the Effects of Participation in Three Types of Appraisal Interviews," *Journal of Applied Psychology*, 83 1 (1973), pp. 54-59.

19. T. R. Mitchell, "Motivation and Participation."

20. A. S. Tannenbaum and F. H. Allport, "Personality Structure and Group Structure: An Interpretive Study of Their Relationship Through an Event-Structure Hypothesis," *Journal of Abnormal and Social Psychology*, 53 (1956), pp. 272-280; V. H. Vroom, "Some Personality Determinants of the Effects of Participation," *Journal of Abnormal and Social Psychology*, 59 (1959), pp. 322-327.

21. K. E. Runyon, "Some Interactions Between Personality Variables and Management Styles," *Journal of Applied Psychology*, 57, 3 (1973), pp. 288-294.

22. T. R. Mitchell, C. R. Smyser and S. E. Weed, "Locus of Control."

23. R. J. House, "Notes on the Path-Goal Theory of Leadership" (University of Toronto, Faculty of Management Studies, May 1974).

24. R. S. Schuler, "Leader Participation, Task Structure and Subordinate Authoritarianism (unpublished mimeograph, Cleveland State University, 1974).

Chapter 7

CONTRACTING FOR LEADERSHIP STYLE: A PROCESS AND INSTRUMENTATION FOR BUILDING EFFECTIVE WORK RELATIONSHIPS

Paul Hersey

Kenneth H. Blanchard

Ronald K. Hambleton

The concept of *Management by Objectives* (MBO) was first introduced by Peter Drucker in the early 1950's. Since its introduction MBO has grown rapidly in popularity throughout the world. Through the work of George Odiorne,[1] John Humble[2] and others,[3] managers in many types of organizational settings—industrial, educational, governmental and military—have been attempting to run their organizations with the MBO process as an underlying management concept. Unfortunately, MBO success stories have not occurred as often as anticipated by theorists who have written about MBO or by practitioners who have applied it. Why?

There has been a major missing link to more successful implementation of MBO: contracting for leadership style.[4] In most MBO programs, an effort is made for managers and their subordinates to reach agreement only on performance goals; there is little attention given to developing "contracts" between managers and their subordinates regarding the role of managers in helping subordinates accomplish the negotiated objectives.

Management by Objectives

Management by Objectives, as it is practiced in most organizations, begins with an agreement among superiors and subordinates on the common goals of the entire organization. At this time, any changes needed in the organization's structure—for example, changes in title, duties, or span of control—are made. Next, each superior and subordinate independently proposes time-oriented goals for the subordinate's job and the methods to be used to evaluate on-the-job performance. These are discussed and jointly agreed on by the superior and the subordinate. Also, checkpoints are established. These are times when a superior and a subordinate will compare together the performance goals with what has actually been accomplished; any necessary adjustments are made—and inappropriate goals discarded. At the end of the time period, a final mutual review of objectives and performance takes place. If there is a discrepancy between the two, efforts are initiated to determine what steps can be taken to overcome problems. This sets the stage for a determination of objectives for the next time period.

The entire cycle of *Management by Objectives* is represented graphically in Figure 1.[5]

The Missing Link

The special aspect of MBO, as compared to many other management systems, is that superiors and subordinates participate in the establishment of performance goals *and* in the evaluation that takes place in relation to the agreed-upon goals. It has been found that participation in the formulation of objectives tends to make subordinates feel more personal responsibility for goal attainment and is thus more effective than having objectives imposed by an authority figure in the organization. The problem with MBO—and a reason why few effective implementations occur—is that the role of the manager in helping subordinates accomplish objectives is not usually specified.

We believe that MBO would be a powerful tool for productivity improvement if superiors negotiated with subordinates the leadership style most useful to help subordinates meet objectives just as the superiors

Figure 1
THE CYCLE OF
MANAGEMENT BY OBJECTIVES

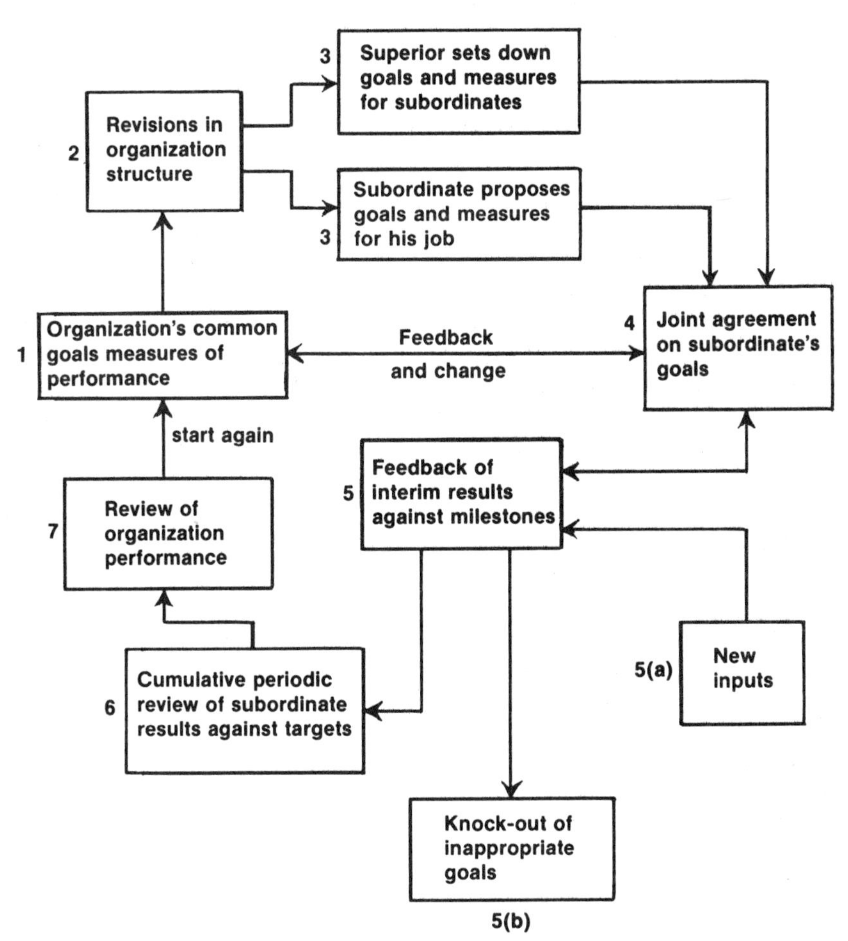

negotiate job objectives. As golfers, with the aid of their caddies, select a club depending on the ball's lie on the course, so managers, with the help of their subordinates, should select the leadership style to be used in achieving the agreed-upon objectives. *Situational Leadership* developed by Paul Hersey and Kenneth H. Blanchard[6] should help in this selection.

The primary purpose of this paper is to integrate Situational Leadership with MBO by showing how managers and their subordinates can contract for leadership styles with respect to job objectives. The paper is divided into three sections: (1) a review of Situational Leadership, (2) a description of the development of an instrument and scales to measure follower maturity, and (3) a discussion of the use of the maturity scales to facilitate contracting for leadership style.

Situational Leadership

Situational Leadership is a management theory developed by Hersey and Blanchard to help people—whether they be managers, consultants, administrators, teachers, trainers or parents (anyone trying to influence the behavior of others)—be more effective in their everyday interactions with others. The theory is based on the amount of direction (task behavior) and the amount of socio-emotional support (relationship behavior) a leader must provide given the situation and "the level of maturity" of the follower or group. The theory can be applied effectively to groups as well as individuals; however, henceforth we will discuss its application in relation to a single subordinate.

Task Behavior and Relationship Behavior

The recognition of task and relationship as two critical dimensions of a leader's behavior has been an important part of management research over the last several decades. These two dimensions have been labeled various things ranging from "autocratic" and "democratic," to "employee-oriented" and "production-oriented."

For some time, it was believed that task and relationship were either/or styles of leadership and, therefore, could be shown as a continuum, moving from very authoritarian leader behavior (task) at one end to a very participative leader behavior (relationship) at the other end.

In more recent years, the idea that task and relationship were either/or leadership styles has been dispelled. In particular, extensive leadership studies at Ohio State University[7] questioned this assumption and showed that other assumptions were more reasonable and would lead to more useful theories of leadership.

By spending time actually observing the behavior of leaders in a wide variety of situations, the Ohio State staff found that they could classify most of the activities of leaders into two distinct and different behavioral categories or dimensions. They named these two dimensions "Initiating Structure" (task behavior) and "Consideration" (relationship behavior). Definitions of these two dimensions follow:

Task behavior is the extent to which a leader engages in one-way communications by explaining what each follower is to do as well as when, where, and how tasks are to be accomplished. *Relationship behavior* is the extent to which a leader engages in two-way communication by socio-emotional support, "psychological strokes," and facilitating behaviors.

In the leadership studies mentioned, the Ohio State staff found that leadership styles tended to vary considerably. The behavior of some leaders was characterized mainly by their directing activities for their followers in terms of task accomplishment, while other leaders concentrated on providing socio-emotional support through personal relationships between themselves and their followers. Still other leaders had styles characterized by both task and relationship behavior. There were even some leaders whose behavior tended to provide little task or relationship for their followers. No dominant style appeared. Instead, various combinations were evident. The observed patterns of leader behavior can be plotted on two separate and distinct axes as shown in Figure 2.

Figure 2

Four Basic Leader Behavior Styles

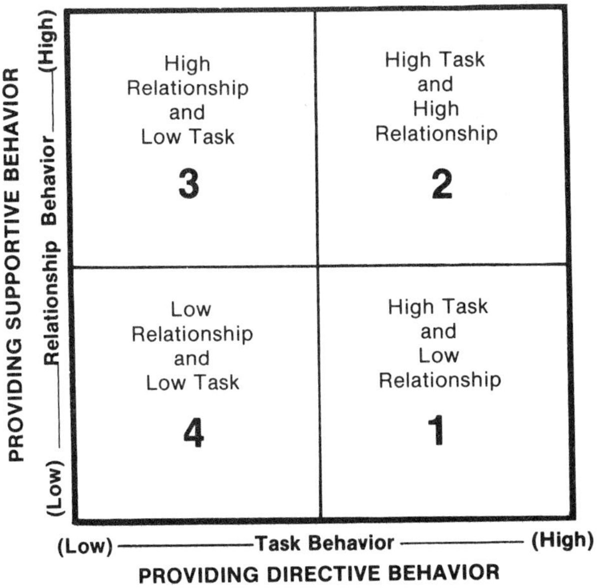

PROVIDING SUPPORTIVE BEHAVIOR (Low) — Relationship Behavior — (High)		
(High)	High Relationship and Low Task **3**	High Task and High Relationship **2**
(Low)	Low Relationship and Low Task **4**	High Task and Low Relationship **1**

(Low) ——— Task Behavior ——— (High)

PROVIDING DIRECTIVE BEHAVIOR

Since research in the past several decades[8] has clearly supported the contention that there is no "best" style of leadership, any of the four basic styles shown in Figure 2 may be effective or ineffective depending on the situation.

Situational Leadership Theory is based upon an interplay among (1) the amount of direction (task behavior) a leader gives, (2) the amount of socio-emotional support (relationship behavior) a leader provides, and (3) the "maturity" level that followers exhibit toward a specific task, function, or objective that the leader is attempting to accomplish through the individual or group (follower(s)).

Level of Maturity

Maturity is defined in Situational Leadership as the willingness and ability of a person to take responsibility for directing his or her own behavior. *These variables of maturity should be considered only in relation to a specific task to be performed.* That is to say, an individual or a group is not mature or immature in any *total* sense. People tend to have varying degrees of maturity, depending on the specific task, function, or objective that a leader is attempting to accomplish through their efforts.

Thus, a sales representative may be very mature in the way he or she approaches sales calls but may not demonstrate the same degree of maturity in developing and writing customer proposals. As a result, it may be quite appropriate for this individual's manager to provide little direction and help on sales call activities, yet provide a great deal of direction and close supervision over the individual's proposal-writing activity.

Components of Maturity

In examining the components of maturity, several comments should be made. First, when we talk about the maturity of individuals as their willingness (motivation) and ability (competence) to take responsibility for directing their own behavior in a particular area, we are suggesting that the general concept of maturity really involves two factors: *psychological maturity* and *job maturity.*

Psychological maturity is related to the willingness or motivation to do something. Individuals who have high psychological maturity in a particular area of responsibility think that responsibility is important and have self-confidence and good feelings about themselves in that aspect of their job. They do not need extensive "patting on the back" or encouragement to get them to do things in that area. A comment from a person high in psychological maturity relative to some job objective might be:

> I really enjoy that aspect of my job. My boss doesn't have to get after me or provide any encouragement for me to do that part of my job.

Job maturity is related to the ability or competence to do something.

Individuals who have high job maturity in a particular area of their work have the knowledge, ability and experience to do tasks in that aspect of their job without the need for direction from others. A person high in job maturity perhaps would say:

> My talent really lies in that part of my job. I can work on my own in that area without much help from my boss.

If persons are divided into high and low levels on each factor for *each* job objective, four combinations arise that can be used to describe persons:

(1) Individuals who are *neither willing nor able* to take responsibility (low on both psychological and job maturity);
(2) individuals who are *willing* but *not able* to take responsibility (high psychological maturity but low job maturity);
(3) individuals who are *able* but *not willing* to take responsibility (high job maturity but low psychological maturity); and
(4) individuals who are *both willing and able* to take responsibility (high on both psychological and job maturity).

The highest level of maturity for an individual or group (in our terms) would be combination 4; the lowest level would be combination 1.

The Basic Concept

According to Situational Leadership Theory, as the level of task maturity of the follower increases, the leader should begin to *reduce* task behavior and *increase* relationship behavior. This should be the case until the individual reaches a moderate level of maturity. As the follower moves into an above-average level of maturity, the leader appropriately decreases not only task behavior but relationship behavior as well. At this point the follower is mature not only in terms of the task but also is psychologically mature.

Since the follower can provide his or her own "strokes" and reinforcement, great socio-emotional support from the leader is no longer necessary. People at this maturity level see a reduction of close supervision and an increase in delegation by the leader as a positive indication of trust and confidence. Thus, Situational Leadership Theory focuses on the appropriateness or effectiveness of leadership styles according to the *task relevant maturity* of the follower(s). This cycle can be illustrated by a bell-shaped curve superimposed upon the four leadership quadrants, as shown in Figure 3.

Style of Leader vs. Maturity of Follower

Figure 3 portrays the relation defined by Situational Leadership between task relevant maturity and the appropriate leadership styles to be used as a

Figure 3
SITUATIONAL LEADERSHIP THEORY

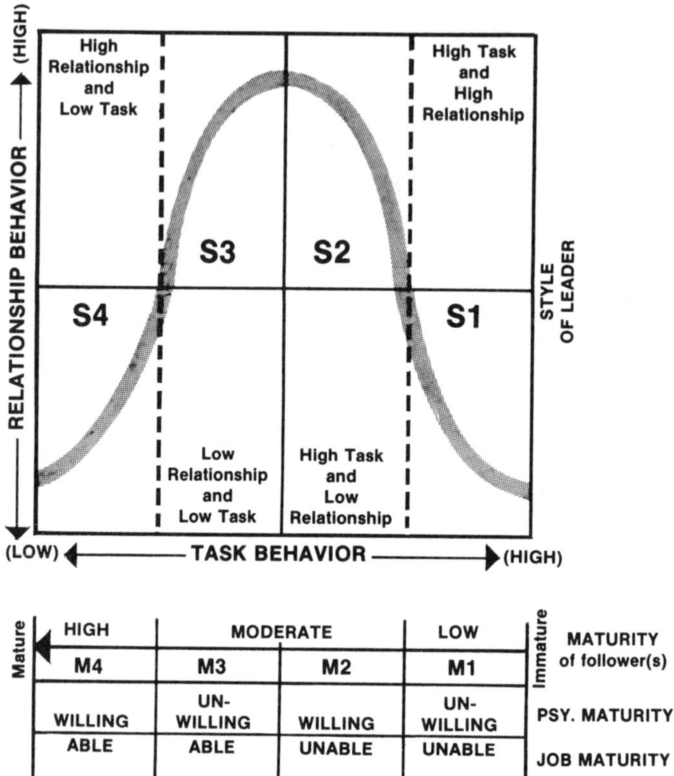

follower moves from an immature to mature state. As indicated, the reader should keep in mind that the figure represents two different phenomena. The appropriate leadership style (*style of leader*) for given levels of follower maturity is portrayed by the curved line running through the four leadership quadrants. (An example is provided later in this section.) The maturity level of the individual or group being supervised (*maturity of followers*) is depicted below the leadership model as a *continuum* ranging from low-level to high-level maturity.

In referring to the leadership styles in the model, we use the following shorthand designations: (1) high task-low relationship will be referred to as leader behavior style S1; (2) high task-high relationship behavior as leader behavior style S2; (3) high relationship-low task behavior as leader behavior style S3, and (4) low relationship-low task behavior as style S4.

In terms of follower maturity, it is not simply a question of being mature or immature but a question of degree. As can be seen in Figure 3, some benchmarks of maturity can be provided for determining appropriate leadership style by dividing the maturity continuum into four levels of maturity. The maturity level of a person who is: (1) unwilling and unable (low on both psychological maturity and job maturity) will be referred to as maturity level M1; (2) willing but not able (high psychological maturity but low job maturity) will be referred to as maturity level M2; (3) able but not willing (high job maturity but low psychological maturity) will be referred to as maturity level M3; and (4) able and willing (high on both psychological maturity and job maturity) will be referred to as maturity level M4.

Application

What does the bell-shaped curve in the style-of-leader portion of the model mean? It means that as the maturity level of one's followers develops along the maturity continuum from immature to mature, the appropriate style of leadership moves accordingly along the curvilinear function.

Determining Appropriate Style

To determine what leadership style is appropriate to use in a given situation, one must first determine the maturity level of the follower in relation to a specific task that the leader is attempting to accomplish through the follower's efforts. Once this maturity level is identified, the appropriate leadership style can be determined by constructing a right angle (90° angle) from the point on the continuum that identifies the maturity level of the follower to a point where it intersects on the curvilinear function in the style of leader portion of the model. The quadrant in which that intersection takes place suggests the appropriate style to be used by the leader in that situation with a follower of that maturity level. Let us look at an example in Figure 4.

Suppose a manager has determined that a subordinate's maturity level in terms of administrative paper work is low. Using Situational Leadership Theory she would place an X on the maturity continuum as shown in Figure 4 (above M1). Once the manager had decided that she wanted to influence the subordinate's behavior in this area, the manager could determine the appropriate initial style to use by constructing a right angle from the X drawn on the maturity continuum to a point where it intersects the curve (designated in Figure 4 by 0). Since the intersection occurs in the S1 quadrant, it is suggested that when working with this subordinate who

Figure 4
DETERMINING AN APPROPRIATE LEADERSHIP STYLE

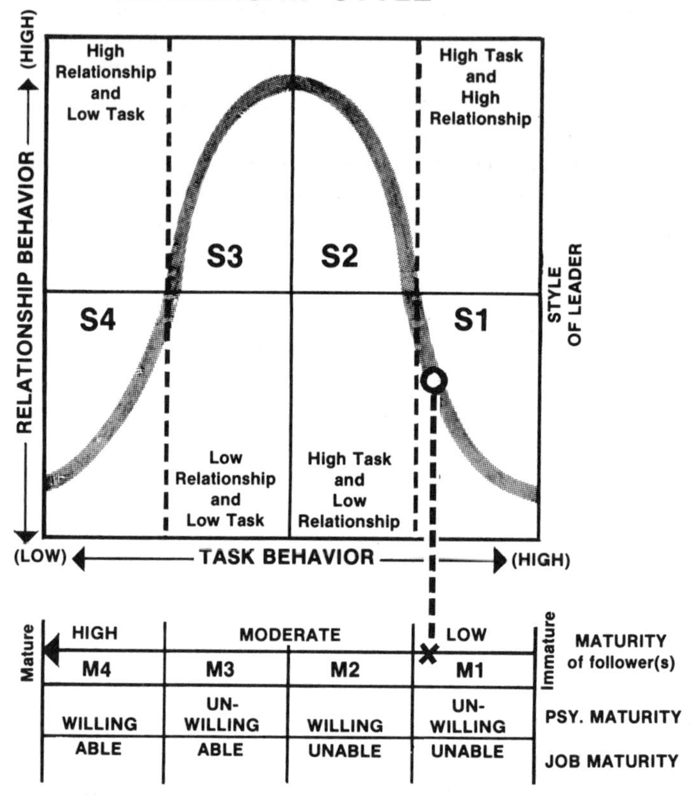

demonstrates M1 maturity on this particular task, the manager should use an S1 style (high task-low relationship behavior). If one follows this technique for determining the appropriate leadership style for all four of the maturity levels, it will become clear that the four maturity designations (M1, M2, M3, M4) correspond to the four leadership behavior designations (S1, S2, S3, S4); that is, M1 maturity requires an S1 style, M2 maturity requires an S2 style, etc. When we say "low relationship behavior," we do not mean that the manager is not friendly or personable to the subordinate. We merely suggest that the manager, in supervising the subordinate's handling of administrative paper work, should spend more time directing the person in what to do and how, when, and where to do it, than providing socio-emotional support and reinforcement. Increased relationship behavior should occur when the subordinate begins to demonstrate the ability to handle necessary administrative paper work. At that point, a movement from Style 1 to Style 2 would be appropriate.

Thus, Situational Leadership Theory contends that in working with people who are low in maturity (M1) in terms of a specific task, a high task/low relationship style (S1) has the highest probability of producing effective results; in dealing with people who are of low to moderate maturity (M2), a moderate structure and socio-emotional style (S2) appears to be most appropriate. In working with people who are of moderate to high maturity (M3) in terms of a specific task, a high relationship/low task style (S3) has the highest probability of producing effective performance. Finally, a low relationship/low task style (S4) is the most likely style to maximize job performance with people of high task relevant maturity (M4).

While it is important to keep in mind the definitions of task and relationship behavior given earlier, the labeling of the four styles of Situational Leadership Theory, when they are being used effectively, as in Figure 5, is sometimes useful for quick diagnostic judgments:

High task/low relationship leader behavior (S1) is referred to as "telling" because this style is characterized by one-way communication in which the leader defines the roles of followers and tells them what, how, when, and where to do various tasks.

High task/high relationship behavior (S2) is referred to as "selling" because with this style most of the direction is still provided by the leader. He or she also attempts through two-way communication and socio-emotional support to get the follower(s) psychologically to buy into decisions that have to be made.

High relationship/low task behavior (S3) is called "participating" because with this style the leader and follower(s) now share in decision making through two-way communication and much facilitating behavior from the leader because the follower(s) have the ability and knowledge to do the task.

Low relationship/low task behavior (S4) is labeled "delegating" because the style involves letting follower(s) "run their own show." The leader delegates because the follower(s) are high in maturity, being both willing and able to take responsibility for directing their own behavior.

It is important to emphasize that *the labels "telling," "selling," "participating" and "delegating" should only be used to describe an effective use of styles S1, S2, S3, and S4*. For example, when style S4 is used inappropriately with a person who has low maturity in a particular work area, that would not be called "delegating." It would be more abdication than delegation, thus would not be given the same label as the effective use of Style 4.

Figure 5
SITUATIONAL LEADERSHIP

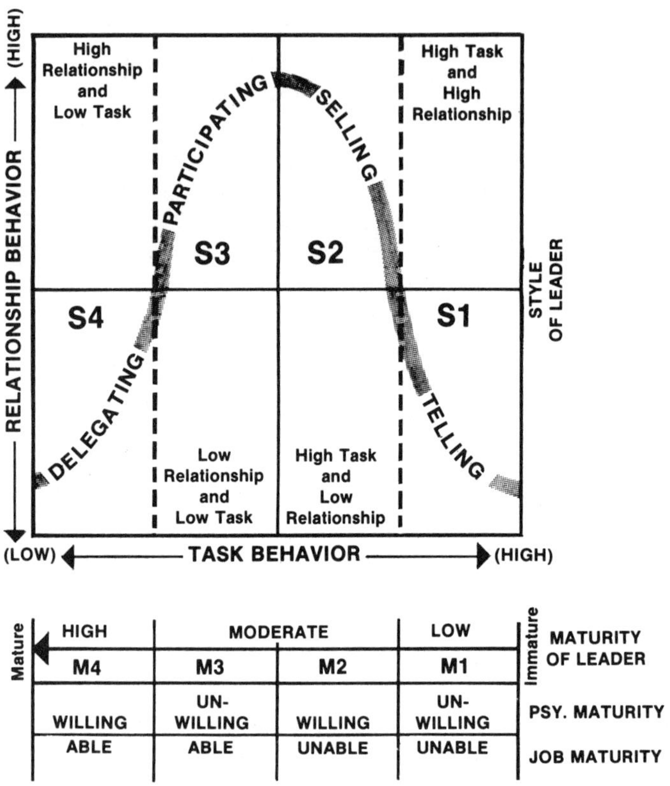

(HIGH) ← RELATIONSHIP BEHAVIOR → (LOW)

High Relationship and Low Task
High Task and High Relationship
PARTICIPATING
SELLING
S3
S2
S4
S1
DELEGATING
TELLING
Low Relationship and Low Task
High Task and Low Relationship
STYLE OF LEADER

(LOW) ← TASK BEHAVIOR → (HIGH)

Mature	HIGH	MODERATE		LOW	Immature	MATURITY OF LEADER
	M4	M3	M2	M1		
	WILLING	UN-WILLING	WILLING	UN-WILLING		PSY. MATURITY
	ABLE	ABLE	UNABLE	UNABLE		JOB MATURITY

Situational Leadership and MBO

In most MBO programs, once a superior and a subordinate have agreed upon certain goals for the subordinate and how the accomplishment of those goals can be measured, it is common for the superior to move to a S4 style (low relationship/low task) in supervising the subordinate until the next check point. According to Situational Leadership, for this movement to an S4 style to be effective, the subordinate involved must be both willing and able (maturity level M4) to direct his or her own behavior to accomplish each of the agreed-upon objectives. Clearly, such a situation does not always exist. Most people are at different maturity levels on their various job objectives. That is to say, there are some aspects of their job for which they may be either inexperienced or unmotivated or both. As a result, we feel that once goals and objectives are established between a superior and his or her subordinate, the next logical step (but not often used) is for both parties involved—the superior and subordinate—to negotiate the appropriate leadership style that the superior will use in helping the subordinate accomplish each objective. If contracting for leadership styles does not take place, problems may occur. For example, if the superior leaves the subordinate completely alone, the superior will be unaware until the next interim check period whether this low relationship/low task leadership style (S4) is appropriate ("delegating") or inappropriate ("abdication"). An S4 style would be effective for accomplishing objectives only in areas where the subordinate has significant technical skill and know-how. Conversely, if, after negotiating goals and objectives, a leader continually hovers over and directs the activities of a subordinate, this high task/low relationship style (S1) might alienate subordinates who are competent and capable of working alone.

Development of an Instrument to Measure Maturity

If a leader and a follower are to agree upon an effective leadership style that the leader should use with the follower, both of them must be able to determine accurately the maturity level of the follower on each of his or her job objectives. To help managers and their followers make "valid" judgments about follower maturity, and thereby facilitate their agreement on appropriate leadership styles, we have recently developed two different maturity instruments—the Manager's Rating Form and the Self-Rating Form.[9]

The Manager's Rating Form

The first maturity instrument that we developed was the Manager's Rating Form. In developing this form, one of our first decisions was to consider maturity as a two-dimensional construct. As we discussed earlier, maturity consists of both the *willingness* (motivation) and *ability* (competence) of a person to direct his or her behavior while working on a particular job objective or assuming a particular responsibility. Willingness and ability are referred to, in our work, as *psychological maturity* and *job maturity*, respectively.

Our next step was to generate a long list of possible rating scales to "tap" each of the two dimensions. For example, with the job-maturity dimension we produced scales such as "past job experience," "job knowledge" and "understanding of job requirements." For the psychological-maturity dimension, scales such as "willingness to take responsibility," "commitment," and "achievement motivation" were devised. In total, we produced about 30 scales as potential indicators of each dimension. These scales were later edited and revised by a group of managers and by us. The most relevant 20 scales measuring each dimension were selected for further study. Corresponding to each scale, we then produced "behavioral indicators" of the end points.

JOB MATURITY SCALES

This person .... in performing this objective

SCALES	High		Moderate				Low	
	8	7	6	5	4	3	2	1
	M4		M3		M2		M1	
1. Past Job Experience	Has experience relevant to job						Does not have relevant experience	
	8	7	6	5	4	3	2	1
2. Job Knowledge	Possesses necessary job knowledge					Does not have necessary job knowledge		
	8	7	6	5	4	3	2	1
3. Understanding of Job Requirements	Thoroughly understands what needs to be done					Has little understanding of what needs to be done		
	8	7	6	5	4	3	2	1

PSYCHOLOGICAL MATURITY SCALES

This person .... in performing this objective

SCALES	High		Moderate				Low	
	8	7	6	5	4	3	2	1
	M4		M3		M2		M1	
1. Willingness to Take Responsibility	Is very eager						Is very reluctant	
	8	7	6	5	4	3	2	1
2. Achievement Motivation	Has a high desire to achieve					Has little desire to achieve		
	8	7	6	5	4	3	2	1
3. Commitment	Is very dedicated							Is uncaring
	8	7	6	5	4	3	2	1

For example, with the scale "past job experience," the end-points of the scale were chosen to be "has experience relevant to job" and "does not have relevant experience." With the psychological maturity scale "willingness to take responsibility," the end-points of the scale chosen were "is very eager" and "is very reluctant" and so on.

As the examples above also reveal, eight-point rating scales are used in the instrument. Low to high designations correspond to our M1 to M4 maturity benchmarks. Thus, ratings of 1 or 2 correspond to maturity level M1, ratings of 3 or 4 to maturity level M2, ratings of 5 or 6 to maturity level M3, and ratings of 7 or 8 to maturity level M4.

Next, we conducted four pilot studies using the instrument.[10] The data collected in each study were analyzed with such techniques as item analysis and factor analysis. In addition, we assessed the reliability of scores derived from the instrument. The results of these pilot studies can be summarized as follows: (1) we were able to select the most appropriate scales (7 in all) from the initial pool of scales to measure each dimension, (2) we determined that leader ratings on as few as five scales in each dimension were sufficient to produce acceptable score reliability, and (3) we improved the readability and clarity of instrument directions and score interpretations.

In our most recent research on the maturity instrument, we had each of 51 managers rate one of his employees. The manager rated the same employee twice, using the same job objectives on each occasion. The time interval between the two occasions varied from a few hours with some managers to about three days for others. In total, the 51 managers rated their employees on 224 job objectives. (Typically, a manager rated an employee on four or five job objectives.)

The test-retest reliability of the job-maturity scores (across managers and job objectives) was .84. For the psychological-maturity scores, the test-retest reliability was .88. Clearly, there was substantial consistency in the ratings of employees on particular job objectives on both occasions. Of course, the time period between occasions was short, but if the time between occasions were lengthened, reliability estimates would be influenced by both inconsistency in manager ratings *and* real changes in employee maturity levels. The influence of this second source of variation would lead to biased estimates of reliability of the job- and psychological-maturity scores.

Even more interesting than our results on the reliability of job- and psychological-maturity scores are our results on the percent of agreement, on the two occasions, in the determination of a leadership style for an employee on a particular job objective. The percent of agreement was over 77%. This result means that over 77% of the time a manager made the same selection of a leadership style in a retest administration (after a short period of time) of the maturity instrument. Since the primary use of the maturity instrument is to help a leader determine the highest-probability-of-success leadership style in a particular situation at a given time, it is extremely important to know what level of agreement there is in the determination of a leadership style in two parallel administrations of the instrument. (Incidentally, leaders did not know they were going to be asked to repeat their ratings of a follower on a second occasion.) A figure of 77% agreement is quite high and could be expected to be even higher if managers receive some training in completing the instrument. The managers in our study had no prior training or experience with the instrument. Therefore, our reliability results are probably conservative estimates of the results that can be achieved when managers are properly trained to use the instrument.

How the Manager's Rating Form is Used

A manager completing the maturity instrument on a subordinate is first asked to identify the most important objectives this subordinate has for his or her job. If the superior and subordinate are involved in an MBO program, the objectives for the subordinate would already have been negotiated between the two. If these objectives are to be really useful, and tangible, easily measurable indicators of accomplishment should also have been specified for each objective.

Once these objectives have been established, the manager is asked to select the five (5) *most relevant Job Maturity scales* (from the 7 provided) and the five (5) *most relevant Psychological Maturity* scales (from the 7 provided) for each of the established objectives and then "rate" the maturity level of each subordinate separately on each established objective, using the scales that have been chosen. A manager does not have to choose the same job maturity and psychological maturity scales for each of the job objectives rated. Thus, the manager may decide that the scales most relevant for one objective are not the same ones that are most relevant for a different objective.

Managers are given a choice of rating a subordinate on any five of the seven job maturity scales and any five of the seven psychological maturity scales for two reasons: (1) It gives the manager some choice because not all dimensions will apply to every objective the manager wants to rate, and (2) in our work to date with the maturity scales we have found that a manager's overall rating of a subordinate on particular objectives does not change significantly whether he or she uses only five scales (no matter which five he chooses) or all seven of the scales. This was also true during earlier development phases when many more than seven were available from which to choose.

Once a manager has completed the ten ratings on a particular objective, a job maturity score and psychological maturity score for that objective are obtained by adding the total of the job maturity ratings and the psychological maturity ratings. The highest possible score for job maturity or psychological maturity is 40 and the lowest possible score is 5.

Once job maturity and psychological maturity scores are calculated, these scores are used with the interpretation matrix shown in Figure 6 to determine both the subordinate's overall maturity level (with respect to a particular job objective) and the most appropriate leadership style (or combination of styles) as perceived by the manager.[11]

Figure 6
Interpretation Matrix
DATA MATRIX

PSYCHOLOGICAL MATURITY				
M4	S2 Job 5 to 12 Psy 33 to 40 M2	S2/3 Job 13 to 22 Psy 33 to 40 M2/3	S3/4 Job 23 to 32 Psy 33 to 40 M3/4	S4 Job 33 to 40 Psy 33 to 40 M4
M3	S2 Job 5 to 12 Psy 23 to 32 M2	S2/3 Job 13 to 22 Psy 23 to 32 M2/3	S3 Job 23 to 32 Psy 23 to 32 M3	S3/4 Job 33 to 40 Psy 23 to 32 M3/4
M2	S1/2 Job 5 to 12 Psy 13 to 22 M1/2	S2 Job 13 to 22 Psy 13 to 22 M2	S2/3 Job 23 to 32 Psy 13 to 22 M2/3	S2/3 Job 33 to 40 Psy 13 to 22 M2/3
M1	S1 Job 5 to 12 Psy 5 to 12 M1	S1/2 Job 13 to 22 Psy 5 to 12 M1/2	S2 Job 23 to 32 Psy 5 to 12 M2	S2 Job 33 to 40 Psy 5 to 12 M2
	M1	M2	M3	M4
	JOB MATURITY			

Follower maturity and the most appropriate leadership style for a particular objective are determined by locating the box in the matrix which contains the combination of *job maturity* and *psychological maturity* scores for the follower. In the lower left hand corner of that box is the subordinate's overall *maturity* designation for that objective/responsibility. In the upper right hand corner of the box is the high probability leadership style the manager should use for that maturity level. (In some of the boxes the maturity level and appropriate leadership style are expressed as in between two specific designations.)

Suppose a manager scored a subordinate as 27 in *job maturity* and 24 in *psychological maturity* for a particular objective. According to the data matrix in Figure 6, these two scores would fall in the box where the job-maturity and psychological-maturity scores range from 23 to 32. As suggested in the box, the *overall maturity* for that subordinate for that objective (as perceived by his or her superior) would be M3, and the most appropriate leadership to be used with that subordinate would be S3—participating (High Relationship/Low Task).

The determination of a follower's maturity level and corresponding best leadership style (or combination of leader styles) is repeated for each job objective or responsibility. After some training with the instrument, leaders should be able to complete their ratings on an employee in about ten minutes.

Self-Rating Form

Recently the Manager's Rating Form has been revised slightly so that it can also be used for self-ratings by subordinates. A Self-Rating Form is necessary to initiate a program combining MBO with contracting for leadership style.

Contracting for Leadership Style

Before contracting for leadership style can begin, the first four steps of the MBO cycle (see Figure 1) must be completed. Once a superior and subordinate have agreed upon and contracted certain goals and objectives for the subordinate and have agreed upon measures to evaluate goal accomplishment, the next logical step would be negotiation and agreement about the appropriate leadership style that the superior should use to help the subordinate accomplish each of the objectives. It is at this point that the maturity instruments are used to facilitate this process.

Suppose a salesman and his boss (the district sales manager) agree on several objectives for the year in each of his areas of responsibility—sales, service, administration and team support. After this agreement, if they both were familiar with Situational Leadership, the next step would be the negotiation of leadership style appropriate for helping the salesman accomplish his goals. Using the two maturity instruments, they would proceed as follows:

Independent Assessment

The sales manager would independently complete the Manager's-Rating Form of the maturity instrument on the salesman for each of the agreed upon objectives, while the salesman would do the same on the Self-Rating Form. The sales manager and the salesman could then compare their perceptions of the salesman's level and the appropriate leadership style that the sales manager should use on each of the agreed-upon objectives.

Joint Agreement

The salesman and the sales manager would meet and share their maturity and leadership-style designations. They would discuss one at a time each of the objectives agreed upon for the salesman.

The first step in this process would be to discuss which of the 7 scales each of them used in assessing both *job maturity* and *psychological maturity*. Since they each had to choose 5 out of the 7 scales provided for these two dimensions of maturity, it is possible that they may not have chosen the same scales to rate. Since they would be sharing why they chose each of the scales, this discussion would eliminate any concern about either party choosing the job maturity scales or psychological maturity scales that would make the subordinate look good or bad. This discussion would also give both parties some feedback on what the other person thought were the most relevant aspects of *job maturity* and *psychological maturity* for each of the salesman's objectives. This is information that is often not shared between superior and subordinate.

The second step would be to compare individual maturity and leadership-style designations for each of the agreed-upon objectives to discover any differences in their perceptions about the ability and motivation of the salesman to accomplish these objectives. Where they both agree on the salesman's maturity and the appropriate leadership style, there would not need to be much discussion.

Where there is disagreement between the salesman and the sales manager about the maturity level of the salesman, a discussion to clarify their different perceptions could take place. This would be an opportune time for the salesman to share with his boss any of his past experience or background as well as insecurities and motivations that the sales manager may be unaware of. At the same time, the sales manager could share with the salesman his good feelings as well as concerns about the subordinate's work in sales, service, administration and team support. Through this feedback and disclosure process they should eventually come to agreement on maturity level and appropriate leadership style. If this agreement is difficult to accomplish, we recommend that the superior (in this case the sales manager) go along with the follower's perception. We feel this permissiveness is important, particularly when contracting for leadership styles is first attempted in a particular superior-subordinate relationship. If the boss "wins" all these early disagreements, the subordinate will soon learn to keep opinions to himself or herself and to figure out what the superior wants to hear.

The contracting process that occurs should result in the sales manager's agreement to use a variety of leadership styles in relation to the agreed-upon objectives. Thus, in areas where the salesman is experienced and has been successful in accomplishing similar objectives, like sales volume, the negotiated leadership contract might be for his boss to leave him on his own (S4). In this case, rather than directing and closely supervising behavior, the sales manager would make sure that the resources are available for the salesman's reaching his agreed-upon sales volume and for coordinating sales efforts with other salespersons under the sales manager's supervision. With another goal in an area where the salesman might have little experience, like team support (this is a new job requirement for sales persons in this company), they might negotiate significant supervision and support (S2) from the sales manager until the salesman understands his role in team support and is able to function without help from his boss. With another objective area like service, where the salesman is competent but not highly motivated, the sales manager may agree to give the salesman support and encouragement but little direction (S3). Seldom will a superior and subordinate negotiate an S1 style on a major objective. While the sales manager may want to begin to prepare the salesman to take some responsibility in an area where he is unwilling and unable (Ml), the sales manager would probably not want to set major objectives in this area.

Determining What Each Contracted Style Means

Once the sales manager and his salesman have agreed upon the style of supervision to be used with each objective, the next step in the contracting process is to determine what each contracted style means in terms of the sales manager's behavior. Unless what the two have agreed upon is translated into specific manager behavior, the contracting process may end as only an intellectual exercise. One way to avoid this pitfall is for the salesman and sales manager to sit down with their calendars and set up meetings according to the agreed-upon supervision. In objective areas where an S2 style has been contracted, the sales manager may agree to meet the salesman twice a week for an hour to work on this area with him. In S3 contracted areas he may make an appointment for lunch with the salesman once every several weeks for the salesman's progress reports and for the sales manager's expression of the needed support. And, finally, in S4 areas the salesman would be responsible for calling the sales manager for a meeting if he needs any help or support.

It is obvious from the way we have been discussing the scheduling of meetings that if the sales manager wanted to develop the salesman in an area where he was both unwilling and unable to direct his own behavior (Ml), he would almost have to meet with the salesman daily in the beginning to give him the required direction and supervision.

Writing down these agreed-upon meetings in their calendars will insure that there will be follow through after the initial contracting sessions.

Modifying Levels of Maturity

Once the salesman and his boss have agreed upon what each contracted leadership style means in terms of meetings, the sales manager should be aware of any improvements in the salesman's ability and motivation to direct his own behavior. He can then gradually reduce the frequency and focus of these meetings as the salesman begins to mature. In the beginning, in areas where the salesman is low in maturity, the scheduled meetings will be frequent, structured, and directive (S1). As the salesman begins to develop, the meetings will gradually be less frequent and become more "give and take" (S2), then less frequent and more supportive and non-directive (S3), and eventually these meetings will be called only at the request of the salesman (S4). Note how the sequencing of styles moves forward through the curve depicted in Figure 3. The movement is from "telling" to "selling" to "participating" to "delegating."

In attempting to improve the maturity of followers who have not taken much responsibility in the past, a leader must be careful not to increase socio-emotional support (relationship behavior) too rapidly. If this is done, the followers may view the leader as becoming a "soft touch." Thus, the leader must develop followers slowly using a *little* less task behavior and a *little* more relationship behavior as followers mature. When an individual's performance is low, one cannot expect drastic changes overnight. To obtain more desirable behavior, a leader must reward as quickly as possible the individual's slightest appropriate behavior in the desired direction and must continue this process as the individual's behavior comes closer and closer to the leader's expectations of good performance. This is a behavior modification concept called *reinforcing positively successive approximations.*[12] For example, if the sales manager wants to improve the maturity level of a subordinate so that this salesman will assume significantly more responsibility, the manager's best bet initially is to *reduce* a little of the direction (task behavior) and to give the salesman an opportunity to assume some increased responsibility. If this responsibility is well handled, the sales manager should reinforce this behavior with increases in relationship behavior. This is a two-step process: first, reduction in direction, and, *if adequate performance follows*, second, increase in socio-emotional support as reinforcement. This process should continue until the salesman is assuming significant responsibility and performing as an individual of moderate maturity. This does not mean that the salesman's work will have less direction, but the direction will now be internally imposed by the salesman rather than externally imposed by his boss. This process can be accomplished, as we discussed earlier, by gradually reducing the frequency and focus of meetings between the salesman and sales manager.

When this process occurs, followers are able not only to provide their own direction for many of the activities in which they engage, but they also begin to provide their own satisfaction for interpersonal and emotional needs. At this stage followers are positively reinforced for accomplishments by the leader *not* looking over their shoulder and by the leader leaving them more and more on their own. It is not that there is less mutual trust and friendship (in fact, there is more), but it takes less direct effort on the leader's part to prove it with mature followers.

Managers must learn not only to change their style as subordinates develop their maturity but also when subordinates begin to behave less maturely in an area. Thus, when subordinates' performances begin to decline, for whatever reason—*i.e.*, crisis at home, change in responsibility, etc.—it becomes appropriate and necessary for leaders to adjust their behavior backward through the curve in Figure 3 to meet the present maturity level of the followers. For example, suppose the salesman is working well without much supervision in a particular aspect of his job and is meeting with his boss only when he calls the sales manager. Then, suddenly, a family crisis begins to affect his performance in this area. In this situation, it might very well be appropriate for the sales manager to schedule a meeting with the salesman in which he can increase *moderately* both direction and support (move back to style 3) until the subordinate regains composure. If that does not occur, the sales manager can call more frequent meetings and gradually move back to style 2 or even S1, if necessary.

Important Things to Remember

Several things should be emphasized in discussing the negotiation of leadership style.

Open Contract

The contract for leadership style should be an "open" contract. Once style has been negotiated for accomplishing a particular objective, it can be opened for renegotiation by either party. For example, the salesman may find in a particular aspect of his job that working without supervision is not realistic. At this point, he may contact the sales manager and set up a meeting to negotiate for more direction from him. The sales manager, at the same time, may gather some data that suggest the style being used with the salesman on a particular task is not producing results. The sales manager in this case can ask for a renegotiation of style.

Shared Responsibility

When a boss-subordinate negotiation over leadership style occurs, it implies a shared responsibility if objectives are not met. For example, if the salesman has not accomplished the agreed-upon goals and the sales manager has not provided the contracted leadership style or support, the data then become part of the evaluation of both people. This means that if a boss has contracted for close supervision, he cannot withhold help from a subordinate (even though the boss may be busy on another project) without sharing some of the responsibility for lack of accomplishment of that goal.

Contract Not Always Negotiated

While we have been discussing joint agreement on goals and objectives and appropriate leadership style throughout this paper, we should emphasize that it is not always appropriate for a manager to engage in this joint process. A process through which a superior and subordinate mutually agree upon anything implies a leadership style somewhere between style 2 (telling) and style 3 (participating). And yet, as Situational Leadership implies, this approach may not always lead to the "best" results, particularly with people who are overall at the extremes of maturity. Thus, involvement and participation in goal-setting and contracting for leadership style with people who are "trading time on the job to satisfy needs elsewhere" and are uncommitted to organizational goals (M1) might lead to less than desirable results. Such people see more responsibility as a punishment rather than a reward, and therefore directive leadership (S1)—where they are told what, when, where and how to do things—might have a higher probability of success. At the other end of the maturity continuum—with people who are "confused about the difference between work and play" and are very competent, self-motivated and committed to organizational goals—mutual goal-setting and contracting for leadership style might be considered a "waste of time." Such people know exactly what needs to be done and how to do it, and goal-setting with them might be done best by asking them to send a memo to their boss outlining their goals and objectives and how they will know whether they have accomplished them. A mutual goal-setting meeting may be unnecessary; the boss needs to merely get out of the way. Thus, according to Situational Leadership, mutually agreeing upon objectives and appropriate leadership style with subordinates has a higher probability of success as the maturity of these subordinates moves from low to moderate levels of maturity (M1 to M2 to M3) and then begins to plateau in potential effectiveness as these followers become highly mature.

Example: Contracting For Leadership Styles in a Restaurant

Integrating the negotiation of leadership styles with MBO through the use of the maturity scales is a new process but is already meeting with some initial success in industrial, educational, and service organizations. An example of some interesting results occurred in a small restaurant chain. In many restaurant chains supervisors are expected to spend a certain number of days each month at each restaurant. This visitation policy is dysfunctional for supervisors who recognize that their restaurant managers vary in experience and competence, and therefore have varying needs for supervision from their boss. If a restaurant supervisor decides to schedule visitations according to his perception of the competence of the restaurant managers, problems often occur with managers at either end of the extreme. Left alone, a highly experienced manager may be confused by the lack of contact with the supervisor and may even interpret it as a lack of interest. At the same time, an inexperienced manager may interpret the frequent visits of the supervisor as a sign of lack of trust and confidence. In both cases, what the supervisor does may be interpreted as negative by the managers.

These problems were eliminated in a small restaurant chain when the supervisors and managers were both exposed to Situational Leadership and then, using the two forms of the maturity scales, attempted to negotiate what the supervisor's leadership style should be with each of the restaurant managers on the job. It was found that when a delegating S4 style was generally negotiated between the supervisor and an experienced restaurant manager, because both agreed that this manager was capable of working on his own, infrequent visits from the supervisor were perceived by the manager as a reward rather than a punishment.

The same thing held true at the other end of the continuum. It was found that when negotiation for leadership style took place with an inexperienced restaurant manager, who realized that the supervisory system was designed to help managers learn to work on their own, this manager was less reluctant to share anxieties about certain aspects of his job. If the negotiation led to initial close supervision and direction, the manager was able to view this interaction as positive not punitive because it was a temporary style and demonstrated the supervisor's interest in helping him to operate on his own.

In summary, establishing objectives and reaching consensus over performance criteria in a traditional MBO program tend to be appropriate for working with subordinates of moderate maturity. If this negotiation procedure is combined with a similar process for negotiating the appropriate leadership style that a manager should use to facilitate goal accomplishment in a specific task area, this additional procedure may help to make the process of MBO more a developmental one, which can be effective in working with all levels of maturity.

NOTES

1. George S. Odiorne, *Management By Objectives: A System of Managerial Leadership* (New York: Pitman Publishing Corp., 1965).

2. John W. Humble, *Management By Objectives* (London: Industrial Education and Research Foundation, 1967).

3. See also J. D. Batten, *Beyond Management By Objectives* (New York: American Management Association, 1966); Ernest C. Miller, *Objectives and Standards Approach to Planning and Control*, AMA Research Study '74 (New York: American Management Association, 1966); and William J. Reddin, *Effective Management By Objectives: The 3-D Method of MBO* (New York: McGraw-Hill Book Company, 1971).

4. This concept of a missing link was first discussed by Paul Hersey and Kenneth H. Blanchard in "What's Missing in MBO " *Management Review*, October 1974, pp. 25-32. This paper builds upon that article by significantly updating the Hersey-Blanchard Situational Leadership concept, presenting and discussing two new scales for measuring the maturity level of an individual and explaining how these instruments can be used to enhance the contracting-for-leadership-style process.

5. Odiorne, *Management by Objectives.*

6. Situational Leadership Theory (formerly referred to as Life Cycle Theory of Leadership) was developed by Paul Hersey and Kenneth H. Blanchard at the Center for Leadership Studies, Ohio University, Athens, Ohio. It was first published by those authors as "Life Cycle Theory of Leadership" in *Training and Development Journal*, May 1969. The theory has continually been refined until in this present form it is referred to as Situational Leadership. The most extensive discussion of this concept can be found in Hersey and Blanchard, *Management of Organizational Behavior*, 3rd edition (Englewood Cliffs, N.J.: Prentice-Hall, Inc., 1977).

7. Roger M. Stogdill and Alvin E. Coons, eds., *Leader Behavior: Its Description and Measurement*, Research Monograph No. 88 (Columbus, Ohio: Bureau of Business Research, The Ohio State University, 1957).

8. As examples see John K. Hemphill, *Situational Factors in Leadership*, Monograph No. 32 (Columbus, Ohio: Bureau of Educational Research, The Ohio State University, 1949); Fred E. Fiedler, *A Theory of Leadership Effectiveness* (New York: McGraw Hill Book Company, 1967); William J. Reddin, "The 3-D Management Style Theory," *Training and Development Journal*, April 1967, pp. 8-17 and *Managerial Effectiveness* (New York: McGraw-Hill Book Company, 1970).

9. These two scales were developed by Ronald K. Hambleton, Kenneth H. Blanchard, and Paul Hersey through a grant from Xerox Corporation. We are grateful to Xerox Corporation not only for providing financial support for the instrument development project, but for allowing us to involve many of their managers and employees in our development and validation work. In particular, we would like to acknowledge Audian Dunham, Warren Rothman, and Ray Gumpert for their assistance, encouragement and constructive criticism of our work. The instruments are available through the Center for Leadership Studies, 230 West Third Avenue, Escondido, CA 92025.

10. See R. K. Hambleton, K. H. Blanchard, and P. Hersey, "Development and Validation of an Instrument to Measure Maturity," *Laboratory of Psychometric and Evaluative Research Report No. 59*, and "Validity of Situational Leadership Theory and Applications," *Laboratory of Psychometric and Evaluative Research Report No. 60.* (Amherst, Mass.: School of Education, University of Massachusetts, 1977.)

11. Research on the adequacy of the interpretation matrix has been underway for some time. Preliminary evidence provides substantial support for entries in the matrix.

12. For classic discussions of behavior modification, reinforcement theory or operant conditioning, see B. F. Skinner, *Science and Human Behavior* (New York: The Macmillan Company, 1953) and *Analysis of Behavior* (New York: McGraw-Hill Book Company, 1961).

Chapter 8

PERSON-TASK FIT AND LEADERSHIP STRATEGIES

Thomas W. Johnson

John E. Stinson

How can I be a more effective leader? What can I do to keep people from being "turned-off?" How can I motivate my people more effectively? These are questions we continually hear in our work with managers and executives in all types of organizations.

Unfortunately, we have found no simple answers. There is no list of "10 steps to effective leadership" that we have found to be useful. The simplistic search for the "one best style" of leadership has been more confusing than helpful.

Rather, it has become increasingly apparent that leadership is situational: leader actions that are effective in one situation may not work in a different situation. The first-line supervisor may work differently with subordinates than the President of the company. Two first-line supervisors in different departments may have to function quite differently. The same manager may have to work differently with different subordinates.

Most recent researchers on leadership have recognized the importance of context and have concentrated on the search for important situational variables. Factors such as the maturity of followers, the nature of the task performed by followers, the amount of power possessed by the leader are but a few examples of situational variables that have been investigated. While a number of important situational variables have been identified, no one approach or theory has provided all the answers.

With the risk of adding to the confusion, we have been investigating another situational variable—one we call person-task fit. In this paper we will examine worker reactions to their tasks. Then we will suggest alternative leadership strategies for different person-task fits.

Person-Task Fit

Much of the interest in the impact of tasks on individuals' job attitudes and behavior has been stimulated by the work of Frederick Herzberg and his colleagues.[1] In their original study they interviewed 200 engineers and accountants. They asked the interviewees to think of times when they felt particularly good and times when they felt particularly bad about their jobs. The engineers and accountants were then asked to describe the factors that led to these particular feelings.

When talking about particularly bad times, the engineers and accountants brought up things such as unfair company policies, poor relationships with their boss and co-workers, and low pay. In contrast, when asked about particularly good job experiences, they generally did not mention these factors. Rather, they talked about recognition they had received for a well done job or the opportunity their jobs gave them for personal growth and development.

Herzberg and others repeated these interviews with a variety of workers in different types of organizations. The results were generally the same. From these studies, Herzberg developed the two-factor theory of motivation.

According to Herzberg, the absence of certain job factors tends to make workers dissatisfied. However, the presence of these same factors does not, in and of themselves, produce high levels of motivation. They merely help avoid the problems created by dissatisfaction—absenteeism, turnover, and grievances. Herzberg called these factors maintenance factors. They include:

- fair company policy and administration
- a supervisor who knows the work
- a good relationship with one's supervisor
- a good relationship with one's co-workers
- fair salary
- job security
- good working conditions

To build high levels of motivation and job satisfaction, a different set of factors is necessary. However, if these factors are not present, their absence does not lead to strong dissatisfaction. Herzberg called these motivator factors. They include:

- the opportunity to accomplish something significant
- recognition for significant accomplishments
- the opportunity to grow and develop on the job
- the chance for increased responsibility
- the chance for advancement

Although maintenance factors had long been considered the key to motivation by many managers, Herzberg advocated job enrichment as a motivation strategy. He argued that building in motivator factors and making the job more challenging was the key to improved motivation and job attitudes.

In contrast to Herzberg's line of thought, some have questioned the value of job enrichment as a general-purpose motivational strategy. They argue that individual responses to job characteristics are heavily influenced by individual differences and that, therefore, only some workers can be expected to respond positively to job enrichment. Among the first to articulate this point of view were Turner and Lawrence.[2] In a study conducted in eleven firms, Turner and Lawrence explored the relationship between job complexity and work attitudes. They found that small town workers responded positively to more complex tasks. Surprisingly, the opposite was true for urban workers. They were dissatisfied by complex jobs and preferred simple, less challenging work.

Additional support for these findings was obtained by Hulin and Blood.[3] In urban areas, correlations between job level (roughly analogous to job complexity) and job satisfaction were positively related. For white collar workers the nature and location of the community seemed to make no difference; job level and job satisfaction were positively related.

A somewhat different approach was initiated by Hackman and Lawler.[4] They suggest that it is the level of desire for higher order (growth) need satisfaction that shapes individual's reactions to jobs. Their research indicates that when jobs provide increased opportunity for personal discretion and learning, people with high needs for growth respond more positively to the work than do people with weak growth needs. A number of recent studies have produced similar findings, and it now appears that measures of human needs are a useful way to tap the differences among people that affect their reactions to jobs.[5]

Utilizing previous research, George Strauss has developed a scheme for categorizing jobs and people and making predictions about responses to work.[6] He classifies jobs into those that are complex and those that are simple (using complexity to include factors such as autonomy, structure, variety, and opportunity to participate). Strauss categorizes people in terms of their motivational orientation toward work. He identifies two basic types of motivational orientation—expressive and instrumental. Individuals with expressive orientations are high-need achievers who are attempting to obtain self actualization *through their work*. (They are similar to Hackman and Lawler's high-need-for-growth individuals). Those with an instrumental orientation look upon their job merely as a means to an end. They are not attempting to actualize the self through work; they are more concerned with external rewards.

Considering the different types of motivational orientation and different types of jobs, one can identify different situations in terms of person-task fits as shown in Figure 1. For each of these situations we can make predictions about worker performance and job attitudes.

Two of the situations are potentially stable; there are good fits between the individual and the task. These include Situation 2 and Situation 4. In Situation 2 we find individuals who seek fulfillment of growth needs on the job and are fortunate enough to hold a job where this is possible. In the absence of any significant environmental interference (such as extremely difficult working conditions, inadequate resources, or pronounced problems with other maintenance factors), we can expect fairly high levels of performance and positive job attitudes.

This is true, however, only for individuals with sufficient skills and abilities to perform the task. While it has long been recognized that motivation and ability are both necessary for superior performance, recent discussions of worker reaction to jobs have tended to focus exclusively on motivation. We believe that Situation 2 is inherently stable only for those who have the necessary abilities to perform their complex job. Those who lack ability are underqualified for the task (Situation 2a), and their motivation to grow and develop is likely to sow the seeds of frustration and failure—perhaps to the point where their motivation is undermined.

Situation 4 is also potentially stable. In Situation 4 we find instrumentally oriented individuals who work on realistic, simple jobs. Individuals with an instrumental orientation work simply to earn a living and view their job only as a means to this end. They do not want to fulfill higher order needs on the job. They are not motivated to do more than "a fair day's work for a fair day's dollar". However, as long as management provides maintenance factors such as adequate pay, reasonable working conditions, and fair supervision, they will not be actively dissatisfied with their job and will perform at an acceptable level. Further, ability is not generally a problem since simple jobs require very limited skills.

The other situations are inherently unstable. In Situation 1 are people who are faced with greater challenge than they want, people who are

Figure 1
Person-Task Fit for Different Situations

MOTIVATIONAL ORIENTATION	TASK Simple	TASK Complex
EXPRESSIVE	SITUATION 3. Individual overqualified for task	SITUATION 2. High ability individual balanced person-Task Fit SITUATION 2a. Low ability individual individual underqualified for task.
INSTRUMENTAL	SITUATION 4. Balanced. Person-task fit.	SITUATION 1. High ability individual individual underqualified for task. SITUATION 1a. Low ability individual individual underqualified for task.

underqualified because of motivational orientation. They prefer to trade time for money and become minimally involved with job-related decisions. But, they are in jobs which are quite demanding.

Here again, however, motivation provides only a piece of the puzzle. Ability must also be considered. Individuals who do not desire challenge and complexity (instrumental orientation) but have the ability to perform may learn to enjoy greater responsibility and change their orientation (moving to person-task fit 2), or, more likely, they may exhibit minimal job performance, dissatisfaction, or even outright rejection by quitting. Nevertheless, for some of these individuals there is hope.

Individuals in Situation 1 without the ability to do the job are underqualified both in terms of ability and motivational orientation. For them the outlook is even bleaker. In all likelihood, they represent a bad placement decision from the point of view of both the individual and the organization. In such situations, there is likely to be inadequate performance, dissatisfaction, frustration on everyone's part, and eventually either termination or resignation.

Situation 3 is also inherently unstable. Here are individuals who want to fulfill growth needs on the job but find themselves in simple, relatively structured jobs; these individuals are clearly overqualified for their jobs. In such a situation, minimal performance and active dissatisfaction are likely. Some may quit. Others may engage in sabotage, fantasy, or other dysfunctional coping mechanisms. Still others may withdraw psychologically from the job, lower their expectations, and change their orientation from expressive to instrumental. In short, rather than exist in an unhappy and psychologically unstable situation, they develop a "punch-in-punch-out" philosophy.

Leader Strategies

What can the leader do? We view the leader's function as a supplementary one. Crucial to satisfaction and motivation to perform is the balance between the individual and the individual's task—the person-task fit. As long as that balance is equal, or nearly so, the leader need take only minimum action—action sufficient to maintain the equilibrium. When there is a poor person-task fit, the leader must adopt much more proactive strategies—strategies designed to increase performance and increase satisfaction. A look at each of the situations permits an examination of potentially effective leadership strategies. We will examine the balanced situations first and then the unstable situations.

Situation 4. In this potentially balanced situation adequate performance and no strong dissatisfaction are expected. The task is simple, perhaps machine-paced, and performance expectations may be standardized. The task itself is not inherently motivating to the individual, but the individual is not striving to satisfy higher level needs on the job.

If performance is adequate, the most appropriate leader strategy is general supportiveness. The leader needs to ensure the continuation of non-task related sources of satisfaction (opportunity for social interaction, good working conditions, and other maintenance factors) in the organization. The leader should provide positive feedback for the adequate performance by letting people know their efforts are appreciated. Further, the leader needs to ensure that there are no changes in environmental conditions that will interfere with the person-task fit. This *General Supportiveness Strategy* should enable the individual to perform his or her job and obtain the extrinsic rewards desired, without interference that will be frustrating or dissatisfying.

If it is desirable to increase performance, the leader might institute an incentive strategy. In the *Incentive Strategy*, the leader ties additional extrinsic rewards (generally money) directly to improvements in performance. This is a feasible strategy, however, only to the extent that the leader has the authority to offer extrinsic rewards that are meaningful to the individual.

Situation 2. In this balanced situation high levels of performance and high levels of satisfaction are expected. The task is inherently satisfying; the individual desires to, and can, fulfill higher level needs through the work. Further, the individual has the ability and is motivated to perform at a high level.

In this situation, the most effective leader strategy is a *Delegative Strategy.* The leader can delegate responsibility for goal accomplishment to the follower. In the delegative strategy the leader needs to ensure goal consensus. Goals which are consistent with organizational objectives must be established. The goals may be established by the leader, follower, or the two in combination, but it is imperative that there is consensus between leader and follower regarding goals. Further, the leader is responsible for monitoring performance to ensure goal accomplishment. Beyond these activities, the leader can remain relatively uninvolved.

Situation 2a. In this unbalanced situation the individual is underqualified for the task. While the individual is motivated to fulfill higher order needs on the job and the job can be inherently satisfying, the individual does not have the ability necessary to perform the task.

In this situation a *Developmental Strategy* by the leader is appropriate. In the developmental strategy, the leader establishes goals and works with the follower, explaining what is to be done and how, when, and where it is to be done. The leader provides a great deal of direction in a coaching or training format. The leader also utilizes contingent reinforcement. That is, as performance improves and ability increases, the leader reinforces improvement by providing rewards that are meaningful to the individual. Although these rewards may vary, they frequently are as simple as recognition, a compliment from the leader on the improvement.

One other component of the developmental strategy is frequently overlooked. When individuals are motivated but lack the skill to perform a task, they tend to feel anxious and frustrated. To minimize the impact of this frustration, the leader needs to provide an atmosphere of supportiveness. The individual needs to feel that, although he or she does not presently have sufficient ability, the leader is willing to help develop the ability.

An alternative strategy, useful particularly when the individual does not seem to have the potential to improve, is the *Placement Strategy.* If the leader has the authority, he can remove the individual from the task and place the worker in another job that is more consistent with his or her ability or remove the employee from the organization.

Another alternative is for the leader to use a *Control Strategy*. The leader can provide explicit directions for the performance of the task, make all significant decisions, and monitor performance closely to ensure that performance is at least adequate. To a significant extent, the leader is actually providing additional task structure for the individual. This strategy is less desirable and is feasible only if the leader has sufficient time to exercise close supervision over an extended time.

Situation 1. In this situation, the problem is more complex for the leader. The individual is underqualified because of a lack of motivation to fulfill higher level needs through the job. While the individual has the ability to perform the complex task, the individual does not want challenging work.

The Placement Strategy is frequently used in this situation. The leader can remove the individual from the task and, perhaps, from the organization. Self-selection often operates in this situation as well. The individual may remove himself or herself from the job and seek a job more consistent with his or her interests.

Another possibility is for the leader to attempt to use a *Performance-Reward Clarification Strategy*. The leader can clarify for the individual the rewards available and help the individual understand the link between good performance and rewards. Since the individual is not motivated by the work itself, the rewards must be extrinsic ones. Thus, this strategy is feasible only if the leader has the authority to provide rewards that are meaningful to the individual.

A third alternative is to use a *Control Strategy*. The leader can provide explicit directions and monitor closely to ensure that performance is at least adequate. As indicated earlier, this strategy requires a great deal of time on the part of the leader and may require sufficient authority to take action if the individual refuses to perform.

Situation 1a. This is the most problematic of the situations in which the leader deals with the underqualified. The individual has neither the skill nor the motivation to perform the complex task. The situation is clearly the result of poor placement. The most obvious leader strategy is a *placement strategy*. The individual can be removed from the task if the leader has the authority. If this is not possible, the leader can attempt to use strategies mentioned for other situations involving the underqualified. A *developmental strategy* may affect ability. The *performance-reward clarification strategy* may affect motivation to perform. But, in all probability, if a *placement strategy* cannot be used, the leader will have to adopt a *control strategy* and hope to obtain at least a minimum level of performance.

Situation 3. In this unbalanced situation, the individual is overqualified for the task. This is the classic problem of the alienated worker, the problem that job enrichment and other job redesign techniques are designed to solve. The individual, motivated to fulfill higher level needs on the job, seeks challenging work but is employed in a position which requires very little ability and provides no challenge.

One strategy is the *Job-redesign Strategy.* The job can be made less structured, and the individual can be given more responsibility for decision making. For this strategy to be feasible, however, several conditions must be met: (1) it must be technically feasible to redesign the job, (2) it must be beneficial from a cost/benefit perspective, and (3) the leader must have the authority to redesign the job. In the numerous cases where these conditions are not met, alternative strategies must be employed.

The placement strategy is frequently appropriate. The individual can be assigned a more complex task, one more consistent with his or her ability and motivational orientation. This keeps a valuable talent in the organization and provides greater satisfaction for the individual. This strategy requires, however, that the leader have the authority to implement the strategy or at least to make recommendations regarding placement.

A second alternative is the performance-reward clarification strategy. The leader can clarify understanding of available rewards and the link between these rewards and adequate performance. The major difficulty with this strategy is that the individual wants to satisfy higher level needs on the job, but the highly simplified work does not offer higher-level-need satisfaction. Thus, for the strategy to work, the individual must be willing to cope with the simple job and accept more extrinsic rewards. This may require some realignment of the individual's motivational orientation, which may not be possible.

Finally the control strategy may be used. The leader can provide explicit directions and monitor closely to ensure adequate performance. Once again, however, this requires substantial time on the leader's part and requires that the leader have the authority to enforce orders in a meaningful way.

Conclusion

Viewing the leader's role as supplementary, we see significant differences in the degree of leader involvement with followers. If there is a good person-task fit, the leader is relatively uninvolved, using either a delegative strategy, a general supportiveness strategy, or an incentive strategy. When there is a lack of fit between person and task, the leader must take a much more proactive role.

For the underqualified follower, depending on whether the individual is underqualified because of motivational orientation or lack of ability (or both), the leader may use a developmental strategy, a performance-reward clarification strategy, a control strategy, or a placement strategy. For overqualified followers, the leader may use a job-redesign strategy, control strategy, performance-reward clarification strategy, or placement strategy. It should be recognized that these proactive strategies are employed to attempt to solve a problem confronting the leader. The extent to which they are effective depends upon the leader's ability to diagnose the problem and utilize an appropriate strategy, the amount of time available to the leader, and the amount of usable authority possessed by the leader.

Figure 2
Leadership Strategies for Different Situations

MOTIVATIONAL ORIENTATION	Task: Simple	Task: Complex
EXPRESSIVE	SITUATION 3. • Job redesign strategy • Placement strategy • Performance-reward clarification strategy • Control strategy	SITUATION 2. • Delegative strategy SITUATION 2a. • Development strategy • Placement strategy • Control strategy
INSTRUMENTAL	SITUATION 4. • General supportiveness strategy • Incentive strategy	SITUATION 1. • Placement strategy • Performance-reward clarification strategy • Control strategy SITUATION 1a. • Placement strategy • Developmental strategy • Performance-reward clarification strategy • Control strategy

NOTES

1. F. Herzberg, B. Mausner, and B. Snyderman, *The Motivation to Work*, (New York: Wiley, 1959).

2. A. N. Turner, and P. R. Lawrence, *Industrial Jobs and the Worker*, (Boston: Harvard Graduate School of Business Administration, 1965).

3. C. L. Hulin, and M. R. Blood, "Job Enlargement, Individual Differences, and Worker Responses," *Psychological Bulletin* 69 (1968), pp. 41-55.

4. J. R. Hackman, and E. E. Lawler, "Employee Reactions to Job Characteristics," *Journal of Applied Psychology Monograph* 55 (1971), pp. 259-286.

5. A. P. Brief, and R. J. Aldag, "Employee Reactions to Job Characteristics: A Constructive Replication," *Journal of Applied Psychology* 60 (1975), pp. 182-186. J. R. Hackman, and G. R. Oldham, "Motivation Through the Design of Work: Test of a Theory," *Organizational Behavior and Human Performance*, 17 (1976), pp. 250-279. H. O. Sims, and A. D. Szilagyi, "Job Characteristics Relationships: Individual and Structural Moderators," *Organizational Behavior and Human Performance* 17 (1976), pp. 211-230. J. E. Stinson, and T. W. Johnson, "Tasks, Individual Differences, and Job Satisfaction," *Industrial Relations* 16 (1977), pp. 315-322.

6. G. Strauss, "Workers: Attitudes and Adjustment," *In The Worker and the Job: Coping with Change*, edited by J. M. Rosow. (Englewood Cliff, N.J.: Prentice Hall, 1974).

Part 4

EXAMPLES OF EFFECTIVE LEADERSHIP

Chapter 9

SUBORDINATE PERFORMANCE PROBLEMS: AN APPLICATION OF SUPERVISORY FEEDBACK AND POSITIVE REINFORCEMENT

Henry P. Sims

Jack Daily is driving home from a two-day seminar on managerial leadership. While he drives, Jack thinks about what went on at the seminar and how he can use the material presented to be a better manager.

Most of the seminar time was devoted to discussion and lecture about certain "leader behaviors." Jack thinks that one of the most important concepts was that a leader can have a *variety* of leader behaviors that are independent of each other. That is, leadership can be described as more than a *single* leader behavior, and a good leader may be "high" or "low" in a number of distinct leader behaviors. Jack finds this concept useful because his previous concept about leadership had been vaguely defined as being "participative" versus "dictatorial," somewhat similar to the old "Theory Y/Theory X" concept.

Although many different types of leader behaviors were discussed, the seminar usually focused on two dimensions that Jack thinks of as "directiveness" and "supportiveness." Several names were brought out that related somewhat to these two dimensions: for example, "consideration" and "concern for people" were similar to "supportiveness." Also, "initiating structure" and "concern for production" seemed to relate to directiveness. In particular, the concept of the "Managerial Grid" was useful to Jack because it taught him that a manager could score high on both "concern for production" and "concern for people."

In general, Jack liked the seminar and found it useful because it stimulated him to think about his own managerial (leadership) style and because he was now able to articulate some concepts that, until now, had been only vague notions. Despite this generally positive feeling, Jack has some doubts about how he will take what he's learned and put it into practice. For the most part, Jack thinks that the new knowledge he has acquired is "nice to know," but he's having some problems in determining precisely how he can use this knowledge to improve the motivation of his subordinates.

Jack has real and specific problems in mind. Jack, an engineering manager, supervises several engineers, architects and draftsmen. In his mind, Jack is contrasting the performance and attitudes of two of his subordinates, Jim Perkins and Fred Jones. Both Jim and Fred are about the same age, have similar engineering educational background, and both have been working for Jack for about two years. The basic ability of both men is about the same, but the contrast in performance, especially recently, has been substantial.

Jim's performance has been on a rising curve; his projects are completed on time, he spends time in developing new skills when needed, and his time at work is efficiently task-oriented. Fred, on the other hand, has had a decline in performance. Fred's time at work involves too much "fooling around" with unimportant tasks, and he has had trouble completing his projects on time. Fred also spends a lot of time "B.S.'ing" with fellow employees. For a short time, Jack thought Fred might be having personal problems outside the office, but he's fairly sure now this isn't the case. Several times, Jack has warned Fred about excessive "socializing" while on the job. These warnings, which have been none too gentle, have had an effect for a few days, but then Fred has backslid into his typical "I-don't-give-a-damn" attitude.

As he drives, Jack is thinking about the contrast between Jim and Fred and how he can use the leadership concepts to bring Fred's performance up to where it should be. In the seminar, there seemed to be an "unwritten prescription" that "concern for people" might be the best motivational strategy. Jack considers the question of whether he has had sufficient "concern for people" when it comes to Fred. He deliberates whether he should use more "consideration" in dealing with Fred. Jack decides to give it a try . . . tomorrow morning he will make a special point to be friendly with Fred. He promises to himself that he will take a greater interest in Fred's personal life and will make a sincere attempt to be sympathetic to Fred's problems. Having made the decision, Jack turns into his driveway with a sense of optimism and relief. He believes the leadership seminar was time well spent, and he is confident that his intention to be more "considerate" to Fred will improve Fred's performance.

Is Jack's decision correct? What will happen to Fred's performance? Will anything happen to Jim's performance?

Analysis: Subordinate Performance Problems

Five Months Later

Jack was scowling as he walked down the corridor towards the office of Sam Cooper, the Personnel Manager. He was running somewhat late today, and he hurried to meet with Sam so that they could attend the monthly luncheon of the Middle Managers Club. Jack was definitely not in a good mood. First, he had trouble starting his car this morning. Then, when he did arrive . . . late, of course . . . he found his secretary was off with the flu. Jack's main problem, however, stemmed from the monthly project status meeting with his boss, Mike Green. Jack knew that the performance of his department regarding "on time" completion of engineering projects was not everything that it should be. The morning meeting with Mike had been lengthy and difficult. In addition to covering the projects in detail, Mike had made no bones about his displeasure with the performance of Jack's department. Jack had an ominous hunch that Mike was considering some drastic changes or shakeups in an attempt to improve on-time project completion.

Jack thought about the situation as he walked down the hall, and he mumbled some very vulgar words to himself. At this point, Jack thought about his decision (five months ago) to be more "considerate" to Fred Jones. Despite the fact that Jack had made a special effort to show more "concern for people" to his subordinates, especially to Fred, performance in the department had not improved. Fred, in particular, was performing at his usual slow and unacceptable level and was spending just as much time as ever socializing with others. Furthermore, somewhat surprisingly, the performance of Jim Perkins had fallen off somewhat.

Jack felt the immediate urgency of the situation because of the morning meeting with Mike Green. He knew he would have to do something, and his inclination at the moment was to administer a gigantic "kick in the—" to both Fred and Jim and to several other subordinates as well. Above all, Jack believed that he had made a mistake in trying to be more "considerate" and he wished that, instead, he had shown more "initiating structure" in the last few months. He concluded that the instructors of that leadership seminar thought they knew a lot about supervision . . . "in theory" . . . but were really not capable of dealing with the realities of *his* situation. Jack and Sam Cooper were good friends, and Jack hoped to discuss the situation with Sam as they drove to the luncheon.

Sam Cooper listened quietly to Jack as they drove to the luncheon. Jack's problems were not new to Sam, since he knew from private conversations with Mike Green that Jack was having trouble with his department's performance. Sam knew that he himself didn't have any brilliant suggestions. Overall, he generally had approved of Jack's attempt to be more "considerate," and he believed that Jack's subordinates were fairly well satisfied with their work. Deep down, however, he had some doubts about Jack's innate capability to organize his department, but he preferred not to talk about this because he and Jack were such good friends. As they pulled into the Holiday Inn parking lot, Sam decided to avoid any direct commentary on Jack's problem. Instead, he said: "Perhaps our luncheon speaker today can give you some ideas. He's a professor from State University who claims to be a 'Managerial and Organizational Psychologist.' The topic of his talk is 'Feedback and Positive Reinforcement.' "

Jack scowled . . . (he had a lot of practice at scowling recently) . . . as an image of an academic "shrink" came to his mind. He snorted as he thought about the professor interviewing and counseling employees in order to make them "happy" at work. Besides, it wasn't too long ago that he had been "burned" at that leadership seminar. Jack had had enough of "theoretical types" . . . he was just trying to survive long enough to get his department back on its feet.

Jack watched as the waiter removed the hardly touched salad from his place. He listened distantly as the president of the luncheon club introduced Dr. Herbert Hanford. Expecting the worst, Jack settled deep into his chair and listened as Dr. Hanford began: "At one time or another, every manager has performance problems with subordinates. Sometimes it's a matter of capability, or, the lack of skill development. In those cases, selection and training are typical remedies that may solve the problem.

However, all too frequently, performance problems relate to a lack of effort on the part of the individual . . . or . . . perhaps to a problem of misdirection or misallocation of effort. That's what I'm here to talk about; how can a manager or a supervisor deal with a problem of subordinate performance that stems from a lack of properly directed effort? Many managers call this a 'motivation' problem. Others call it a problem of 'bad attitudes.' These terms are O.K., but I prefer to call it a problem of behavior . . . perhaps even misbehavior."

Dr. Hanford continued: "Dealing with behavior rather than motivation or attitudes has some advantages. First, we have the problem of trying to observe or measure 'motivation.' The fact is we can't! Behavior, on the other hand, is something that we *can* observe, and we're typically left with a statement like, 'His motivation must be low because his performance is low.' In essence, this is a tautology!"

"Behavior, on the other hand, *can* be observed, and generally, we can relate behavior to performance. Another way of saying this is that we usually can classify behaviors as 'desirable' (*i.e.*, leading *toward* good performance), or as 'undesirable' (*i.e.*, leading *away* from good performance)."

By now, Jack had started to listen with some interest because Dr. Hanford was talking precisely about the problem that bothered him most. Dr. Hanford continued, and most of his focus was on the question of how feedback and "positive reinforcement" could be utilized as an approach to individual performance problems. Jack listened to this part very carefully, and he wondered whether he himself, as a manager, had been providing adequate feedback and positive reinforcement to his subordinates. If the principles that Dr. Hanford described were correct, they might be at least a partial explanation of the performance problems in Jack's department. Jack was definitely interested because Dr. Hanford's comments had an intuitive "common-sense" approach and did not deal with any abstract theory.

At the end of his talk, Dr. Hanford answered several questions, and he gave several examples to illustrate the points he was trying to make. Jack was definitely intrigued, and he asked the following question: "What about the idea of being 'considerate' to subordinates? Will that help to insure subordinate performance?"

Dr. Hanford replied: "First, let's try to define what being 'considerate' is. My interpretation is that the word refers to friendly and supportive interpersonal behavior . . . usually expressed in conversation form, but it can also be expressed through 'body language' or by facial expression." (This definition struck a chord with Jack. He knew that his facial expression transmitted a lot of information and emotion. Jack's wife, in fact, sometimes jokingly said he was extremely "transparent.") Dr. Hanford continued: "The classical form of being considerate is, of course, giving someone a compliment."

"In terms of facilitating performance, consideration, in itself, is neutral. That is, in some situations, consideration can facilitate performance; in other situations, consideration can retard performance. The important point to remember is this: consideration (or compliments) should be given when it is *deserved.* It is essential that *consideration be contingent upon good performance*! The converse rule, of course, is that consideration should *not* be given when it is *not* deserved. That is, when performance is not good, compliments and supportive interpersonal behavior should not be shown."

"Giving undeserved compliments will not facilitate the performance of the recipient and may well have adverse effects on other employees. The simple rule of thumb is this: be considerate as a personal reward for good performance. Don't give personal rewards for bad performance." Dr. Hanford went on to draw a little blackboard sketch to explain his concept of "performance-contingent reward behavior" (see Figure 1).

Figure 1
THE LOGIC OF A CONTINGENT CONSEQUENCE

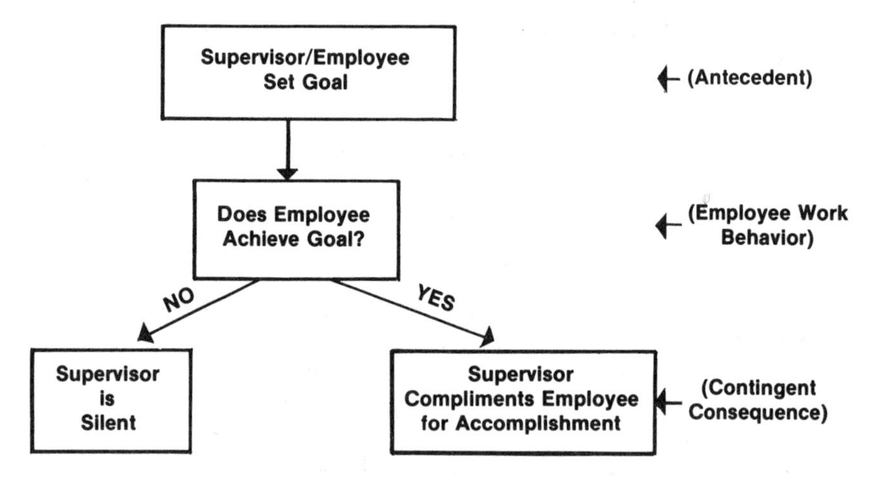

Something clicked in Jack's mind. As a result of the leadership seminar, he had been giving "non-contingent personal rewards" to Fred Jones. As Dr. Hanford had suggested, Fred's performance had not improved, and the performance of Jim Perkins had fallen off. Jack liked Dr. Hanford's common-sense approach, and he decided to learn more.

On the way back to the office, Jack found that Sam shared his enthusiasm for the concepts discussed by Dr. Hanford. Sam agreed when Jack suggested further contact with Dr. Hanford to develop further ideas.

The next day Jack called Dr. Hanford and discussed the possibility of some consulting help for Jack and his department. Dr. Hanford agreed and, as a first step, suggested some readings for Jack to go through before they met.[1] They also agreed to have a first meeting in Jack's office in four weeks. After the conversation, Jack went to the controller's office and made the arrangements for Dr. Hanford's consulting fee. He also ordered the books and articles suggested by Dr. Hanford.

Four weeks later Jack welcomed Dr. Hanford into his office. He noted with some amusement that Mary, his secretary, was somewhat curious about Dr. Hanford. With his full beard and bald head, he did present a rather different, if academic, appearance. Within the four weeks Jack had done his homework well and felt that he had at least a rudimentary understanding of the concepts of feedback and positive reinforcement. Jack realized, however, that putting the concepts into practice would not be as easy as he had originally assumed, and he was hopeful that some specific suggestions would emerge from the meeting.

After some small talk about the championship basketball team at State University, Jack and Dr. Hanford began an in-depth discussion about Jack's department. It was clear to Jack that Dr. Hanford intended to absorb as much background information about the department's functions and objectives as he could within a short time. Jack realized the necessity of this phase of the conversation, and he talked as freely as he could about how the department was run. Dr. Hanford took particular interest when Jack showed him the engineering project control and scheduling system. Jack took particular pride when he described how he himself had developed the scheduling system (which had *not* been in use when Jack took over as manager). Jack maintained and updated the system himself because of its critical importance to managing the department. Jack was enjoying his conversation with Dr. Hanford. As they left for lunch, Jack had the feeling that Dr. Hanford had asked the right questions and had managed to gain quite a lot of information about the department within a short period of time.

At lunch Jack was pleased to note that Dr. Hanford, like himself, was a "salad-man," and they talked for a while about the problem of keeping up a daily jogging routine. As they finished the salads, Dr. Hanford asked about particular problems which, at this time, were critical for the department's effective performance. Jack talked about the problem of achieving "on-time" closure of the engineering projects and, in particular, about the pressure he had recently been receiving from Mike Green. As further examples, he spent time discussing the performance problems of Fred Jones and the recent decline in the performance of Jim Perkins. Dr. Hanford listened intently as Jack went through the situation, interrupting only occasionally to ask a pertinent question. In particular, Dr. Hanford wanted to know, in some detail, how the project scheduling system was used in conjunction with Fred's and Jim's project assignments. This part of the conversation continued with some intensity as they left to return to Jack's office.

After their return to the office, the mode of conversation changed. Previously Jack had done about 75% of the talking, but Dr. Hanford now took the lead. He discussed some general concepts of feedback and reinforcement which he felt applied to Jack's department. Jack had no trouble following Dr. Hanford's train of thought because it was quite similar to the reading that Jack had done in the past few weeks. "First," Dr. Hanford said, "it's important to pinpoint 'target' behaviors. That is, we must be able to identify behaviors that we believe somehow relate to the performance of the department. In essence, we should be able to observe the behavior or at least to see the result or, perhaps, the 'finished product' of the behavior. Second, we have to have some sense as to whether the behavior is *desirable* (*i.e.*, does it contribute to performance?) or, *undesirable* (*i.e.*, does it detract from performance?)."

"Third, we have to be able to *count* and perhaps chart the behavior. Another common way to think of this is to consider the *frequency* of the behavior or how often it occurs over a given time period. These two steps are critical because, as managers, if we are unable to define specific subordinate behaviors that lead to performance, then it would indeed be unrealistic to expect the subordinate himself to recognize exactly what constitutes good performance."

Dr. Hanford continued, "Next, we must analyze the situation in which the behavior occurs. We attempt first to define the antecedents of the behavior. That is, we try to define *what comes before* the behavior. For example, we should ask if the employee knows when a specific behavior is expected, and we should ask if the employee knows how to and has the resources to carry out the behavior. But, more importantly, we should try to do a thorough analysis of the *consequences* of the behavior. We try to answer the question of what occurs *after* the incidence of the behavior."

"We can think of this situational analysis (which, technically is called a *functional analysis*) in the following way; we try to answer two questions: *what comes before* the behavior and *what comes after* the behavior? In analyzing the consequences of the behavior, we try to establish what kinds of reinforcers serve to strengthen the behavior or, conversely, what kinds of penalties (punishments) serve to weaken the behavior?"

"All too often, when we undertake this process the first time, we typically find some unfortunate surprises. Sometimes we find an *absence* of reinforcers to support desired behaviors. Sometimes we find the presence of reinforcers that support undesired behaviors. Remember, our aim is to structure the situation so that we will reinforce the desired behaviors. Alternately, we do *not* want to reinforce the undesired behaviors. In some cases, we may choose to penalize (punish) undesired behaviors, but we should use this approach sparingly and only with conscious deliberateness."

Jack asked, "What happens when we find desired behaviors are not being reinforced or if undesired behaviors are being reinforced?"

Dr. Hanford answered, "Then, we would probably want to attempt a *behavioral change*. The technical term for this is *behavior modification*. That is, we would attempt to *modify* the behavior of the employee. Another way to think of this is *behavioral management*. We attempt to manage the behavior of subordinates by the way we control antecedents and consequences."

"How," asked Jack, "by using consideration?"

"Let me give a cautious *yes* to the part about consideration," said Dr. Hanford. "First, you may recall that my personal definition of consideration was personally rewarding supervisory behavior such as giving compliments or friendly supporting statements. If the so-called consideration is given in response to a desired behavior by the subordinate, it has some possibility of increasing the frequency of the desired behavior. In essence, the administration of personally rewarding supervisory behavior is one approach to behavioral change that has a reasonable chance of success. As a matter of fact, supervisors frequently do not use enough personally rewarding behavior. The most important thing to remember is that this personally rewarding behavior is typically effective only if used *in response to* a desired behavior on the part of the subordinate."

Dr. Hanford went on to discuss several other behavior modification strategies, and he showed Jack a chart listing several kinds of rewards that might reinforce desired behavior in organizational settings (see Figure 2). In addition, he showed Jack a flow chart that detailed the steps to be taken in attempting a behavioral change (see Figure 3). Step by step, he went through the behavioral change process with Jack.

"Last but not least," he continued, "we must continue to measure and chart the frequency of the behavior after we have undertaken the behavioral change strategy. We must use this measurement process if we want to conclude whether the behavioral change strategy has been effective." He further said, "Our expectations shouldn't be too high. It may

FIGURE 2

REWARDS FROM ORGANIZATIONAL ENVIRONMENTS*

Consumables	Manipulables	Visual and Auditory	Tokens	Social	Task and Time	Self-administered
Coffee-break treats	Desk accessories	Office with a window	Money	Friendly greeting	Job with more responsibility	Self-recognition
Free lunches	Wall plaques	Piped-in music	Stock	Informal recognition	Job rotation	Self-praise
Food baskets	Company car	Redecoration of work environment	Stock options	Formal acknowledgment of achievement	Early time off with pay	Self-congratulations
Easter hams	Watches	Private office	Movie and sports passes			
Christmas turkeys	Trophies	Feedback about performance	Trading stamps	Invitations to coffee/lunch	Extended breaks	
Company dinners	Rings		Paid-up insurance	Solicitations of suggestions	Personal time off with pay	
Company picnics	Tie pins		Dinner and theater tickets	Compliment in work progress	Work on personal projects on company time	
After-work parties	Appliances for the home		Vacation trips	Recognition in house organs	Use of company facilities	
Beer parties	Home shop tools		Profit sharing	Pat on the back	Use of company recreation facilities	
	Garden tools			Smile		
	Clothing					
	Club privileges			Verbal and non-verbal recognition and praise		

* Most of these rewards were originally listed by Luthans, F. and Kreitner, R. *Organizational Behavior Modification*, Glenview, Ill.: Scott, Foresman and Company, 1975, p. 101.

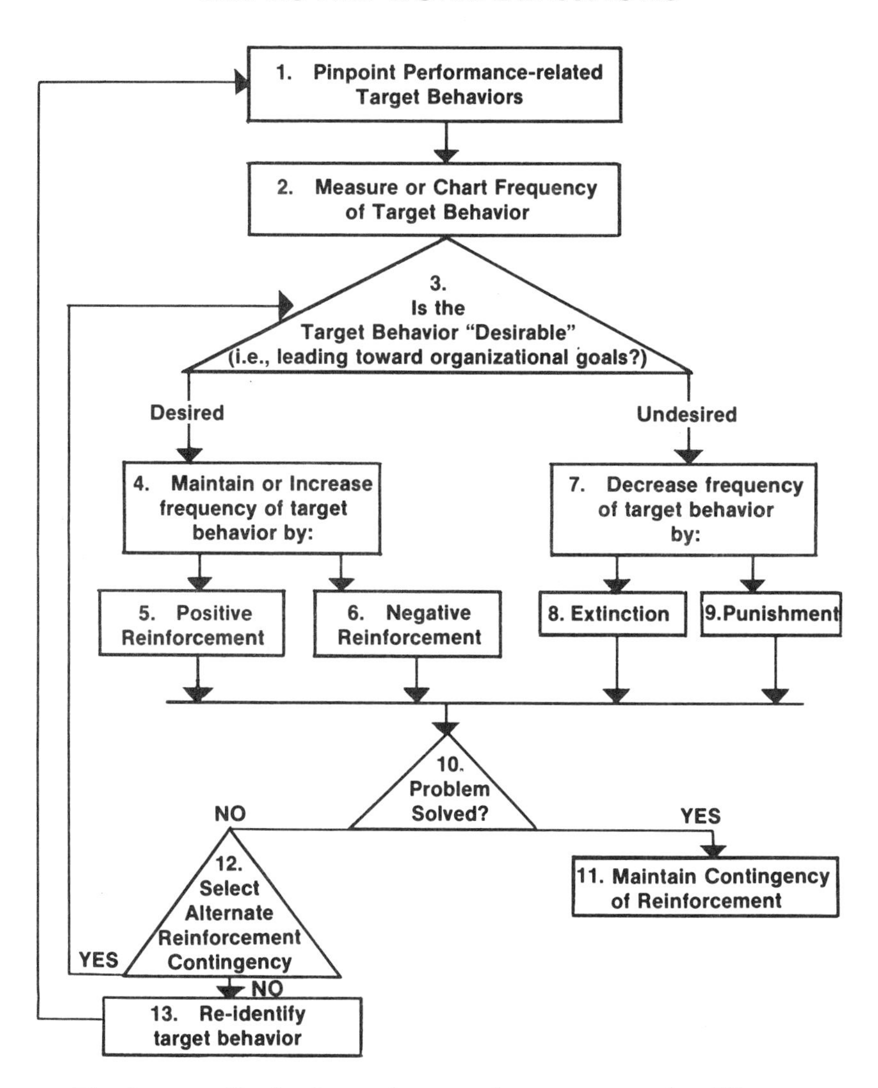

well be that we will miss the mark on our first attempt, and we'll have to go through the process all over again, trying a new behavioral change strategy. Also, as we make the situational analysis, we may well find that some reinforcers are presently beyond our control, and it is indeed possible that an effective behavioral change strategy is not within the control of the manager. Nevertheless, it seems to me that it is incumbent upon a manager to attempt behavioral changes when required. After all, this really is the essence of being a manager . . . organizing or structuring the situation in such a way that subordinate performance is enhanced. The failure to attempt these kinds of behavioral changes would be a failure of managerial responsibilities."

By then it was mid-afternoon. As Jack sipped at his coffee, he decided it was time to get down to the nitty-gritty. "So far, all of this sounds promising. But, as the saying goes, 'It's great in theory, but how can it help me solve my problems?' "

"Well," said Dr. Hanford, "let's start with your two engineers, Jim Perkins and Fred Jones. You've said that Jim is a very capable and skilled engineer and until recently, his performance has been very good. What specific aspect of his performance has recently been lacking?"

"That's easy," said Jack. "Until three or four months ago, Jim completed about 90% of his projects on time. The fact is his on-time completion rate has fallen off."

"Has there been any change in the amount of work he's been given or in the standard by which on-time completion is judged?"

"No," replied Jack. "I'm the one who specifies the due date for each project, and I've been involved in this type of work for almost twenty years. Believe me when I say that I haven't changed the standards on short notice. Once a given level of expertise is attained, the major factor is the attention and effort that the engineer devotes to the work. In the last two or three months, Jim has not given the same amount of effort to his work that had been previously given."

Dr. Hanford said, "Perhaps we should think of 'on-time project completion' as the target behavior that we want to focus on. Is that O.K. with you?"

"Sure."

"We have to keep in mind that there is a danger in this. When we concentrate on completion time, we make the assumption that the quality of engineering work will remain at its present acceptable level. Of course, there is a possibility that if we emphasize completion, engineering quality will suffer as a side-effect. We have to be aware of that possibility and guard against it."

Jack said, "You're right when you say we have to be aware of it and to make sure that engineering quality doesn't fall off. However, let me speculate that this will not turn out to be a problem. Except for the new people, the standard of engineering quality is pretty well recognized. I've never had a serious problem in this respect in the past, but we'll have to watch for it."

Dr. Hanford suggested, "Why don't we get out your project control book and see if we can develop a chart to show exactly what the on-time completion rate has actually been in the past?"

Dr. Hanford and Jack worked with the project control figures for the next 45 minutes. Jack was very receptive when Dr. Hanford suggested some particular kinds of charts. With his engineering background, charts were a natural way for him to analyze a particular situation. After some discussion, Jack and Dr. Hanford agreed that the best time unit was monthly. The chart (see Figure 4) reflected project completion status on the first Monday of each month. Many of the 45 minutes were spent working with the calculator to compile the appropriate statistics. A summary "rough" chart was made to compare overall performance with the performance of Fred Jones and Jim Perkins. It was obvious to Dr. Hanford that Jack's perceptions had not been exaggerated; total performance had indeed been declining, and Jim had also followed the overall trend. Fred's performance was the worst in the department.

Figure 4
CHART OF PROJECT PAST-DUE STATUS

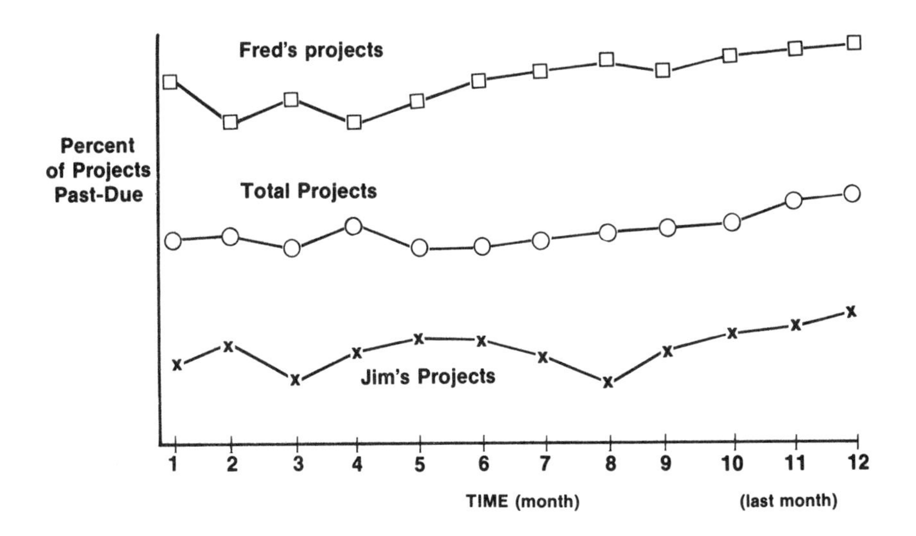

Dr. Hanford asked, "The turning point seems to have occurred about four or five months ago. Do you recall any specific change that took place at that time? For example, was there any change in procedures? Did the overall workload increase?"

"The overall workload has remained about the same," replied Jack.

"Also, I don't recall any specific procedures change or any significant change in the nature of the work. One thing did occur, however, about that time. That was when I went to a two-day seminar on leadership, and I made a special effort regarding my supervisory style when I came back from the seminar."

"What did you do at the seminar?" asked Dr. Hanford. "And how did you change your supervisory style when you came back to work?"

"Well, the seminar leader discussed certain kinds of leadership styles or supervisory styles. We talked about 'initiating structure,' for example, and we also talked about 'consideration.' One of the useful things that I learned was the concept that supervision consists of more than one type of behavior and that a supervisor could be 'high' on both consideration and initiating structure at the same time. No one really said that consideration was a preferred style of leadership, but I somehow came to that conclusion on my own. I recall making a deliberate decision to try to be more considerate of my subordinates. I tried to be especially considerate and supportive of Fred Jones, since he was really a problem employee. I thought my behavior would increase his motivation. I made a conscious effort to avoid 'getting on his back' and tried very hard to be friendly, supportive and complimentary to Fred."

"How did you behave toward Jim?"

"Well, I guess my behavior toward Jim didn't change very much. Jim had always been a very high performer, and I assumed that he didn't need consideration as an 'incentive' like Fred did."

Dr. Hanford asked further, "Was Jim able to observe your behavior toward Fred?"

"Sure. All the engineers work in the same general office area. My interaction with one employee is observed by other employees unless it happens in the privacy of my office. Even then, I doubt if it's a private matter because I know it's common practice to discuss what went on in the boss's office."

Dr. Hanford then asked a perceptive question, "Does this have anything to do with the question you asked me earlier about the effectiveness of consideration as a supervisory style? I remember you asked at the Middle Managers' luncheon if consideration were a useful supervisory behavior."

"That's exactly right," replied Jack. "I'm coming to the conclusion that by giving consideration to Fred, when his performance was bad, that *I may have inadvertently been reinforcing bad performance*. Meanwhile, Jim, who was not receiving the same so-called consideration, was *not being reinforced for good performance*. That may explain why Jim's performance has fallen off while Fred's performance has remained poor. It appears to me that *I may have gotten this thing totally backward*!"

"I think I agree," said Dr. Hanford. "I guess our problem now is what to do about it. Let's try to go back to the general behavioral change concepts that we discussed earlier and apply them to this particular situation. It appears that we have been able to isolate a key target behavior: the on-time completion of engineering projects. In addition, we can measure and record the frequency of the target behavior. What's the next step in trying overtly to increase the frequency of on-time completion? Do you have any any ideas?"

"If we follow the steps that you've outlined," said Jack, "the employee has to know how well he's doing. In this case, each engineer should be given feedback about his actual performance. He should have some idea of what his own on-time completion rate is and he should be able to compare it with others. Perhaps one way to do that would be to compute these charts on a monthly basis and to distribute them to the engineers. We might even post them on a bulletin board in the office. That way, each engineer would be able to keep tabs on his own performance, and he would also have a good idea when his performance is substantially different from the department as a whole."

"Right," said Dr. Hanford. "I think you're getting the right ideas now. In addition to the feedback itself, what about *what comes before* and *what comes after* their behavior on their performance?"

"I think my mind is on track regarding *what comes after* . . . I think you mean what reinforcers will be applied . . . but I'm having trouble following you when you refer to *what comes before*. Let's focus on reinforcers first. It seems to me that my own interpersonal behavior toward each employee would be an immediate thing that could be important. For example, on the day that the monthly charts were posted, I could make it a point to compliment those who have been leaders in on-time completion and also those who have made significant improvements in their on-time completion rate. I would guess that my recognition of these individuals should specifically refer to project completions and should be done so that other individuals might know what's going on. Also, I could perhaps make a practice of taking the leading 'on-time' engineer and, perhaps, the most improved engineer out to lunch that day."

Jack continued, "In addition, as each engineer completes a project assignment, I can make a special point to comment personally on his 'on-time' performance." Jack stopped suddenly then and stared into space for a few moments with a strange look on his face.

"Is something wrong?" asked Dr. Hanford.

"I think there is," said Jack. "How is the engineer to know if he has completed the specific project on time?"

Dr. Hanford asked in return, "How is the target completion date established at the present time?"

"Well, when I make the assignment, I make an estimate of the amount of work required, then I consider the other work that has been assigned to the engineer. Actually, I come up with the final target date myself and enter it into my project control book. I've been doing this for many years, so I believe my target date is not too unrealistic."

"But doesn't the engineer know what the target date is?"

"No, I've always felt the engineer didn't need that information. Except for my boss, I'm the only one who knows what the target date is. It's finally occurring to me that this procedure may have been part of my problem."

"Exactly," said Dr. Hanford. "This is part of what I mean when I talk about *what comes before* the behavior. Usually, it helps when the employee has a clear idea of what is expected of him. In this case, the target date becomes a goal for him to shoot for. In technical terms, we call this a *discriminative stimulus* because it is an environmental cue that helps the employee better understand what it takes to be reinforced."

Jack and Dr. Hanford agreed that the target date should be provided to each engineer at the time the job was assigned. Jack balked, however, when Dr. Hanford brought up the idea of letting the engineer specify the target date. Dr. Hanford talked about research that shows that goals are typically more effective when the employee accepts the goals, which he said, was more likely to happen when he specifies the goal himself. Jack pointed out that he had the most experience in the department in terms of being able to estimate how much work was involved in a project. In addition, if Jack set the goals, the goals would be fairly consistent between individuals. Besides, at this point, Jack didn't quite trust Fred, especially, to set realistic goals. He suspected that Fred would deliberately set easy goals in order to make himself look good. Dr. Hanford did not press the point. He felt that a significant improvement could be made by sharing the targets that Jack established with the engineers and by a deliberate reinforcement strategy. It was obvious, however, that he intended to come back to the subject at a much later time.

"How about organizational reinforcers?" asked Dr. Hanford. "Can they be brought into this situation?"

"I would think so," replied Jack. "We do have an annual salary evaluation review, and my recommendation carries a lot of weight with Personnel as to the distribution of merit raises. If I make merit raises contingent upon on-time job completion, I suspect it may have a reinforcing effect on timely job completion. I suspect, however, that it would be a long-term, rather than a short-term, effect. In the short run, I would expect the other steps we've talked about to have a stronger impact."

"You're right," said Dr. Hanford. "In addition, you would have to make it very clear at the time merit raises were given out that the criterion was tied into on-time project completion."

During the afternoon Jack and Dr. Hanford talked about many other aspects of the department's operations. Near the end of the day, Jack asked Dr. Hanford about the problem of Fred Jones' excessive socializing with other employees. Dr. Hanford said, "We should be able to use our process of analysis on this behavior like any other behavior. First, do we know how much he actually is socializing? Is he socializing more than anyone else? It may well be that you are just super sensitive about Fred because his project completion record is bad."

"I admit to the possibility that you suggest," said Jack, "but I really believe my perceptions are right. I think he really does spend too much time 'B.S.'ing' with other people."

In the few remaining minutes, Dr. Hanford suggested that they work out a method to record what Fred's actual behavior was. Dr. Hanford suggested a work sampling technique. Jack's office was adjacent to the engineering working area, and Jack could see the engineers through his office window if he stood up. Dr. Hanford suggested a frequency coding chart on which was written each engineer's name and a coding scheme that specified certain types of work or interpersonal activities. They agreed upon a time during which Jack would unobtrusively record the work activity of each engineer during the next three weeks. The work sampling procedure should give Jack an actual record of the work and interaction pattern of the engineers. If the plan were successful, Jack and Dr. Hanford would know with confidence whether Fred Jones' socializing behavior was truly excessive.

Six Weeks Later

Dr. Hanford settled into the chair in Jack's office as they began their afternoon meeting. "I noticed on the way in that the project scheduling charts are on your bulletin board. How is it working out?"

"It's too early really to tell," replied Jack. "At least I haven't had any major complaints yet, and one or two people have even told me that they like the idea of posting the project completion target dates. I think it will really be a few months before I'll be able to detect any changes in terms of on-time completions. It will take that long before the lag times can be overcome."

"How about your problem with Fred Jones? Is he still socializing as much as ever? Did you have a chance to do your unobtrusive observation and chart the results?"

"I've completed a chart," answered Jack. "Here's a copy of the results (see Figure 5). I made up a special chart for your visit showing Fred's behavior frequency and comparing his with the average of the other people

I sampled. You can see that my intuitive conclusions were correct. Fred has spent more time socializing than the other people in the department."

Figure 5
CHART OF PERCENT "SOCIALIZING" BEHAVIOR

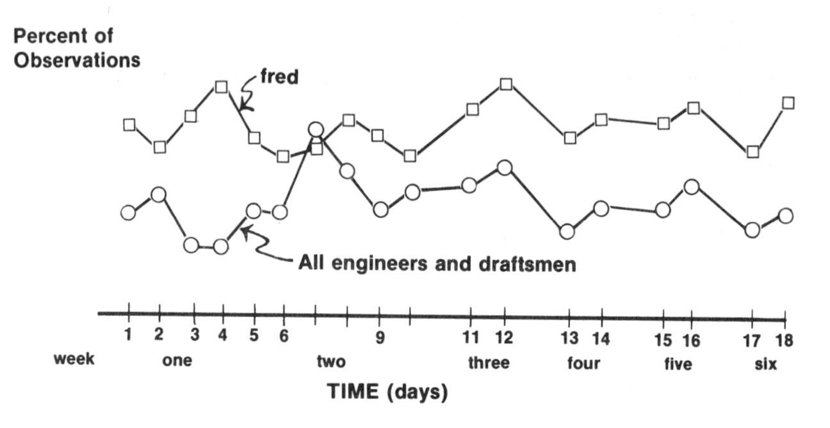

Dr. Hanford asked, "Can we review again how you collected this data?"

"Sure. You'll remember that we decided to take a sample observation on the average of twice an hour for about 15 to 16 observations per day. I worked out a procedure to select randomly the observation time around a mean of a half hour, and I set my wrist alarm to sound at that time. When an observation time came, I merely stood up and casually observed the people in the office and classified their activity according to one of the categories shown on the chart. At the end of the day, I was able to compute a percentage frequency for each category. As it turned out, I wasn't able to do 15 observations each day because I was out of the office sometimes and because sometimes I had someone in my office that prevented me from making the observation. However, I was able to get about 11 or 12 observations a day. I did it every day for two weeks, and, when I saw a pattern emerging, I cut the observation days down to twice a week to see if any significance changes had taken place. We can see that the pattern is fairly consistent over the six weeks."

"I think this has been done very well," said Dr. Hanford. "The technical term for what you have done is called charting a baseline period. The next step is to decide what type of intervention strategy is to be used. But, first, do you have a clear idea what target you want to work on?"

"It's clear in my own mind. Specifically, what I would like to do is to reduce the frequency of Fred's talking to other engineers and draftsmen at their desks."

"Are you sure that talking to other engineers is all that bad?" asked Dr. Hanford.

"Not in moderate amounts," replied Fred. "Each engineer has a particular technical expertise; it helps to be able to share that experience on occasion with another engineer. This is a particularly important way that our new people learn from our more experienced engineers. The critical question is: How much is too much? In my own mind, I'm convinced that Fred's socializing has been excessive and detrimental to his overall work performance. I'm sure I would like to be able to reduce it."

"Let's consider some specific behavioral change strategies. How about punishment or negative reinforcement?"

"If threatening him is a form of negative reinforcement, then I've tried that. I've also tried to punish him by giving him a reprimand when I see him doing too much talking. I get a short-term improvement, but it doesn't last very long. It seems to make him angry, too, and he becomes surly for a while."

"How about extinction?" asked Dr. Hanford. "What would you say are the events that reinforce Fred for his socializing behavior?"

"I would guess that the main reinforcing event that sustains the behavior is the attention that he gets from the other engineers. When he approaches their desks, they respond by talking to him and giving him the attention that he wants. Also, through the observation, I've become aware that the majority of his socializing behavior is concentrated on two or three specific individuals."

Dr. Hanford suggested, "Perhaps you could ask those two or three individuals to make an effort to cut down on socializing with Fred. If you explain the situation to them, they may be willing to cooperate by confining their conversations with Fred to only important work-related subjects."

"Won't Fred know about what I'm doing then?"

"Yes, he will. You might even tell him directly what you are doing. At least it will be an expression of your serious concern."

"Well," said Jack, "that sounds like it's worth a try. It might work. In a positive vein, I must say that I detect a slight difference in Fred after posting the project completion target dates and the overdue project charts. However, it hasn't shown up on any of my charts yet."

One Year Later

Jack greeted Dr. Hanford warmly as they met for lunch at Dante's Italian Restaurant. After an exchange of small talk, Dr. Hanford asked,

"Well, how is the project scheduling system going? Has on-time project completion improved at all?"

"Yes, it has," replied Jack. "Our percent of projects overdue has been reduced considerably. I would say that it's now within a reasonable limit. I guess that I would have to give the main credit to the idea of sharing target goals with the engineers, along with the feedback of the actual results. It's quite apparent to me that these data are of considerable interest to the engineers and tend to have significant impact on their desire to close their projects. As a side effect, I have had quality problems with one engineer. In order to meet time deadlines, he had some instances of incomplete or shoddy work."

"How did you handle that?" asked Dr. Hanford.

"Well, first, I went through some of his past projects and did a subjective rating of each project, of poor, fair, good, or excellent. Unfortunately, he had some projects that were "poor," and some that were "fair," and only one that was "excellent." Then, I called him into my office and went over each of the projects and the rating on each project. I tried to be as explicit as I could about the specific reasons behind my rating of a project. Finally, I told him that I would be providing him with a quality rating on each future project. We agreed that he should shoot for no "poors" and that 85% should be "good" or "excellent." I also was specific about saying that the quality of his projects would be an important factor in his merit ratings."

"How has he responded?" asked Dr. Hanford.

"The quality of his work has definitely improved. I believe the greatest value in the whole incident was the specific tips I gave him when I talked about quality rating. It became apparent to me that I had not been giving him the appropriate feedback that he needed to develop on the job."

"How's Fred Jones doing?" asked Dr. Hanford.

"Well, overall I would say that Fred's performance has improved so that his work is now within the acceptable range. Nevertheless, it is clear to me that Fred is not my best engineer, and his work is definitely not as good as Jim's. You may recall that when we first met Jim's work had fallen off slightly. Now, Jim's performance has exceeded his former levels, and he is the best engineer in my department. Despite my efforts to 'motivate' and manage the behavior of the engineers, there are still substantial individual differences. What does your theory say about an employee being 'self-motivated'?"

Dr. Hanford replied, "There certainly are individual differences in the way people respond to the same set of environmental contingencies. First, it may be that Jim really has more native ability than Fred, at least more than you were able to recognize when they were both new employees. But, it also may be that Jim is simply just better at providing his own stimuli and rewards that are effective in managing his own behavior. The technical term for this is 'self-control,' and it means that some individuals are better able to structure their own contingencies of reinforcement. Frankly, we don't know enough about this part of behavior, but it may be the reason that Jim is more effective in managing his own work output than Fred. I believe that, over the next twenty years, this matter of self-control will be one of the most challenging and fruitful areas of research about behavior at work. At any rate, I'm pleased to hear that both Jim and Fred are doing so much better than the last time we met."

Jack replied with some satisfaction, "Thanks for your help."

Key Concepts

Foreword. The concepts expressed in this case are based on the technology expressed in reinforcement, or operant theory, also frequently called behavior modification. Reinforcement theory focuses on the behavior of individuals in an organizational environment and the events in the individual's environment that control, manage, or modify that behavior. Some of the sources for further reading about these concepts are listed below. In addition, the following set of concepts and terms may be useful.

Antecedent is an environmental event that precedes an employee's behavior. A consequence is an event that follows and is contingent upon an employee's behavior.

Avoidance is any behavior by an employee that *prevents* an adverse event from occurring.

Baseline refers to a period of time where a behavior is observed and recorded, usually immediately prior to an intervention treatment.

A *behavior* is any observable and measurable response or act of an individual employee.

A *behavior definition* is a statement of the exact behavior to be observed, which is frequently a target behavior.

Behavior modification is a science of technology that describes practical techniques for producing changes in socially significant behaviors by the control of environmental events.

Behavioral contingency management refers to the management of employee behavior through the systematic control of the antecedents and the consequences of that behavior.

A *chain* is a sequence of two or more behaviors in which each behavior produces a result that becomes a discriminative stimulus for the next behavior. Most behaviors in organizations are clustered into very complex chains.

Charting refers to the use of a chart or graph to monitor a behavior over time. The chart typically consists of the frequency or the intensity of a behavior recorded over a number of time periods (for example, days). Typically, the chart is divided into a baseline period and then a treatment period.

Classical conditioning refers to the use of stimulus events associated with reflexive behavior. Since virtually all employee behavior in organizations is operant (voluntary) behavior, classical conditioning is rare in organizational settings.

A *consequence* is an environmental event that follows an employee behavior. If the consequence increases the frequency of the behavior, then the consequence is reinforcing. If the consequence decreases the frequency of the behavior, then the consequence is punishing.

A *contingency* is the relationship between a behavior and the events (consequences) that follow a behavior, and the events (antecedents) that precede a behavior.

A *contingent delivery of a reinforcer* means that a reinforcing event is administered to an employee only when the specified target behavior has been performed.

Contingency of reinforcement is the sequence of events and behaviors consisting of environmental antecedent event, then employee behavior, and then environmental consequence event.

Continuous reinforcement is a procedure through which a reinforcing event is administered after every behavior.

Deprivation refers to how recently a person has had a reinforcer—the less recently, the more effective the reinforcer. Satiation is the opposite of deprivation.

Desirable behaviors, from a management viewpoint, are those employee behaviors that contribute toward the goals of the organization. Undesirable behaviors are those employee behaviors that detract from the goals of the organization.

Differential reinforcement is a procedure through which a desired behavior is reinforced while other undesirable behaviors are extinguished.

Direct observation refers to the concept that behavior must be observable or measurable if it is to be managed.

Discrimination training refers to reinforcing an employee in the presence of a stimulus, but not reinforcing in the absence of the stimulus.

A *discriminative stimulus* is a stimulus which indicates a specific behavior. In organizations, a discriminative stimulus would cue an employee of what behaviors will be reinforced. It is an environmental event that occurs prior to an employee behavior.

Escape is any behavior by an employee that *terminates* an adverse event.

Event recording is the measurement of a behavior by counting the number of times a discrete behavioral event occurs.

Extinction is the procedure of stopping an environmental event that has followed a behavior in the past, causing a decrease in the future frequency of the behavior.

Feedback refers to providing information to an employee about the quality or quantity of performance.

Fixed interval reinforcement occurs when a reinforcer is administered after an employee behavior and after a fixed period of time has elapsed.

A *fixed ratio reinforcement* occurs when a reinforcer is administered when an employee completes a fixed number of behaviors.

A *functional analysis* is an attempt to identify the events that support and maintain a particular employee behavior. In particular, the antecedents of the behavior and the reinforcing consequences are identified.

Generalization refers to the use of a previously learned behavior in the presence of a new or novel stimulus.

Imitation is the procedure where an employee learns a new behavior by observing others perform the behavior.

Instruction is the procedure where an employee learns a new behavior through a verbal description of the behavior.

Intermittent reinforcement is a procedure where a reinforcing event is administered after a behavior only at certain times.

Interval recording is the measurement of behavior by observing whether or not a behavior occurs during a short time interval.

An *intervention* is the deliberate introduction of an antecedent or consequence event in an attempt to change the behavior of an employee.

The *Law of Contingent Punishment* states that a punishing event will be more effective if it is delivered when, but only when, the particular behavior to be punished occurs.

The *Law of Contingent Reinforcement* states that a reinforcer will be at maximum effectiveness if it is administered only when a desired target behavior has occurred.

The *Law of Immediate Punishment* states that a punishing event will be more effective if it is delivered quickly after the behavior occurs.

The *Law of Immediate Reinforcement* states that a reinforcer will be at maximum effectiveness the more immediately the reinforcer is administered after the target behavior.

The *Law of Punisher Deprivation* states that a punishing event will be more effective if it has not been delivered frequently in the near past.

The *Law of Punisher Size* states that a punishing event will be more effective if it is strong.

The *Law of Reinforcer Deprivation* states that the more deprived a person is of a certain reinforcing event, the more effective that reinforcer will be.

The *Law of Reinforcement Size* states that the larger the amount of any given reinforcer, the more effective that reinforcer.

Learning refers to any change in behavior that has the effect of producing a change in the environment.

Modeling is the process of learning a new behavior by observing some others perform the behavior.

A *negative reinforcer* is an adverse event that, when terminated or prevented by an employee's behavior, increases the frequency of that behavior. Avoidance and Escape are both forms of negative reinforcement.

Operant behavior refers to voluntary behavior by an employee. In contrast, respondent behavior deals with reflexes. Virtually all employee behavior of interest to management is operant behavior. Operant conditioning refers to the management of operant behaviors through the systematic management of the consequences of that behavior.

Operant conditioning is the management (changing) of an employee's target behavior primarily through the alteration of the environmental events (the reinforcing consequences) that follow the behavior.

Organizational behavior modification refers to the management of employee behavior in organizational settings.

Outcome recording is the measurement of the result of a behavior, rather than the behavior itself.

An *overt behavior* is one that is publicly observable and measurable.

Positive reinforcement refers to the administration of a pleasant event after a behavior has occurred, which has the result of increasing the frequency of that behavior.

Premack Principle involves the pairing of an unpreferred (non-reinforcing) employee behavior with a preferred (reinforcing) employee behavior, in order to achieve the preferred behavior.

A *punisher* is any adverse event that follows an employee's behavior that has the effect of decreasing the frequency of that behavior. A punisher can also be the withdrawal of a pleasing event, after an employee's behavior, that decreases the frequency of that behavior.

A *reinforcer* is any event that follows a behavior that increases the frequency of that behavior.

A *reward* is a subjectively pleasant environmental event. A reward becomes a reinforcer if it has the power to increase the frequency of the target behavior.

A *schedule* refers to the timing by which a consequence event is administered following a behavior.

A *self-administered reinforcer* is a consequence that an employee administers to himself. Self-administered reinforcers are important to the concept of self-control.

Self-control is the capability to administer reinforcing consequences to one's self. Self-control refers to an employee managing his/her own behavior through self-manipulation of antecedents and reinforcing consequences.

Shaping is the systematic reinforcement of successive approximations of a behavior until the ultimate behavior is achieved.

Social reinforcers result from interpersonal interaction such as attention, praise, approval, smiles, nods, and physical contact.

A *stimulus* is any event in the employee's environment that is related to the employee's behavior.

Stimulus control refers to the management of an employee's behavior through the use of stimulus events that occur prior to the behavior. Reinforcing control refers to managing behavior through the use of events that occur subsequent to the behavior.

Stimulus generalization refers to the transfer of a behavior to new or novel situations that are somewhat similar to situations where the behavior was originally learned.

A *target behavior* is a specific employee behavior that an organization or a manager desires to manage (modify).

Treatment refers to the method used to change or to manage employee behavior through the control of environmental events.

Variable interval reinforcement occurs when a reinforcer is administered after an employee behavior, and after a variable period of time has elapsed, where the time period varies around some mean.

A *variable ratio reinforcement* occurs when a reinforcer is administered when an employee completes a variable number of behaviors, where the variable number of behaviors varies around some mean.

Author's Note: This fictionalized version of the interpersonal relationships between a manager and subordinate treats leadership as a process of management of subordinate behavior through techniques of feedback and positive reinforcement. For those readers who desire further knowledge of this approach, the following readings are recommended:

Fred Luthans and Robert Krietner, *Organizational Behavior Modification*, (Glenview, Ill.: Scott Foresman and Company, 1975.)

Training, December, 1976, Lakewood Publications, 731 Hennepin Ave., Minneapolis, Minnesota 55403.

Paul L. Brown and Robert J. Presbie, *Behavior Modification in Business, Industry, and Government*. Behavior Improvement Associates, P.O. Box 296, New Paltz, New York 12561.

Chapter 10

MACGREGOR*

Arthur Elliott Carlisle

There is no question that some managers are better organized than others, but how often does one run into a really well organized manager? Not too often! In the course of my work I run into hundreds of managers a year, yet I can think of only one who managed to be superorganized—to the point that he had time to play an enormous amount of golf. As further proof of his organization, about two years after I ran into MacGregor, which incidentally is not his real name, he was promoted to chief of operations at the corporate level—a fact I discovered when I saw his face looking out at me from the financial section of my newspaper above the announcement of his new executive assignment.

My encounter with MacGregor came during a study of the extent to which operating managers actually use participative management techniques in their dealings with subordinates. The problem with an inquiry of this nature is that nearly every manager either says that he uses a participative approach (because isn't that what every good manager does?) or maybe honestly believes that this is his preferred *modus operandi*; in any event, what I was interested in was information about behavior, not about beliefs (pious or otherwise). So I had to develop an indirect approach to interview managers and follow up with some questions directed at the subordinates they supervised. Accordingly, I developed a questionnaire that I used in interviewing more than 100 managers in ten major U.S. and Canadian firms. The first item on the questionnaire asked whether the interviewee held regular meetings with his subordinates; if so, how often

* Reprinted with permission from *Organizational Dynamics*, Summer 1976.

and what was the nature of the matters discussed. Finally, it tried to determine whether subordinates were offered the opportunity to initiate discussion and actively participate in the decision-making process or were merely afforded the opportunity to hear about decisions the boss had made.

MacGregor, who at the time was manager of one of the largest refineries in the country, was the last of more than 100 managers I interviewed. Although the interview had been scheduled in advance, the exact time had been left open; I was to call MacGregor at his office early in the week that I would be in the vicinity and set up a specific date and time.

Here's how that phone call went: The switchboard operator answered with the name of the refinery. When I asked for MacGregor's office, a male voice almost instantly said, "Hello." When I asked for MacGregor, the voice responded, "This is he." I should have recognized at once that this was no ordinary manager; he answered his own phone instantly, as though he had been waiting for it to ring. To my question about when it would be convenient for me to come see him, he replied, "Anytime." I said, "Would today be all right?" His response was, "Today, tomorrow, or Wednesday would be O.K.; or you could come Thursday, except don't come between 10:00 a.m. and noon; or you could come Friday or next week—anytime." I replied feebly, "I just want to fit in with your plans."

Then he said, "You are just not getting the message; it makes no difference to me when you come. I have nothing on the books except to play golf and see you. Come in anytime—I don't have to be notified in advance, so I'll be seeing you one of these days," and he then hung up. I was dumbfounded. Here was a highly placed executive with apparently nothing to do except play golf and talk to visitors.

I took MacGregor at his word and drove over immediately to see him without any further announcement of my visit. MacGregor's office, in a small building at one corner of the refinery, adjoined that of his secretary, who, when I arrived, was knitting busily and, without dropping a stitch, said to me, "You must be Mr. Carlisle; he's in there," indicating MacGregor's office with a glance at a connecting door.

MacGregor's office was large and had a big window overlooking the refinery, a conference table with eight chairs arranged around it (one of which, at the head, was more comfortable and imposing than the rest), an engineer's file cabinet with a series of wide drawers, two easy chairs, a sofa, a coffee table with a phone on it, and a desk. The desk had been shoved all the way into a corner; there was no way a chair could be slipped in behind it, and it was covered with technical journals. A lamp stood on the desk, but its plug was not connected to an outlet. There was no phone on the desk. MacGregor, a tall, slender man with a tanned face, stood by the window

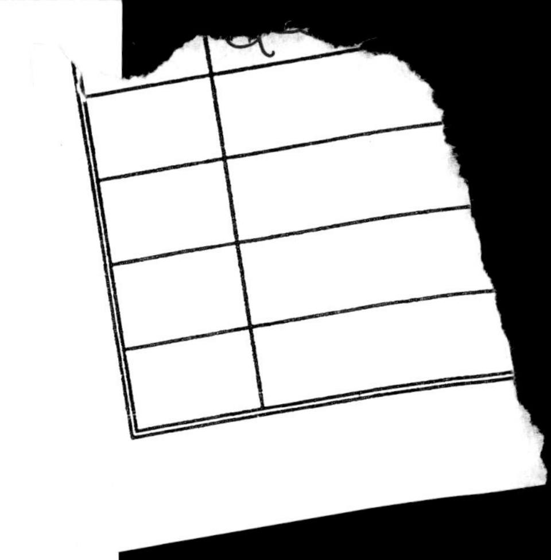

peering absently into space. He turned slowly when I entered his office and said, "You must be Carlisle. The head office told me you wanted to talk to me about the way we run things here. Sit down on the sofa and fire away."

MacGregor's Modus Operandi

"Do you hold regular meetings with your subordinates?" I asked.

"Yes, I do," he replied.

"How often?" I asked.

"Once a week, on Thursdays, between 10:00 a.m. and noon; that's why I couldn't see you then" was his response.

"What sorts of things do you discuss?" I queried, following my interview guide.

"My subordinates tell me about the decisions they've made during the past week," he explained.

"Then you believe in participative decision making," I commented.

"No—as a matter of fact, I don't," said MacGregor.

"Then why hold the meetings?" I asked. "Why not just tell your people about the operating decisions you've made and let them know how to carry them out?"

"Oh, I don't make their decisions for them and I just don't believe in participating in the decisions they should be making, either; we hold the weekly meeting so that I can keep informed on what they're doing and how. The meeting also gives me a chance to appraise their technical and managerial abilities," he explained. "I used to make all the operating decisions myself, but I quit doing that a few years ago when I discovered my golf game was going to hell because I didn't have enough time to practice. Now that I've quit making other people's decisions, my game is back where it should be."

"You don't make operating decisions any more?" I asked in astonishment.

"No," he replied. Sensing my incredulity, he added, "Obviously you don't believe me. Why not ask one of my subordinates? Which one do you want to talk to?"

"I haven't any idea; I don't even know how many subordinates you have, let alone their names. You choose one," I suggested.

"No, I wouldn't do that—for two reasons. First, I don't make decisions, and second, when my subordinate confirms that I don't make decisions, you'll say that it's a put-up job, so here is a list of my eight immediate subordinates, the people who report directly to me. Choose one name from it and I'll call him and you can talk to him," said MacGregor.

"OK—Johnson, then, I'll talk to him if he's free," said I.

"I'm sure he's able to talk to you. I'll call him and tell him you're on the way over." Reaching for the phone, he determined that Johnson wasn't doing anything either and would be happy to have someone to talk to.

Subordinates' Views of MacGregor

I walked over to Johnson's unit and found him to be in his early thirties. After a couple of minutes of casual conversation, I discovered that MacGregor and all eight of his subordinates were chemical engineers. Johnson said, "I suppose MacGregor gave you that bit about his not making decisions, didn't he? That man is a 'gas'."

"It isn't true though, is it? He does make decisions, doesn't he?" I asked.

"No, he doesn't; everything he told you is true. He simply decided not to get involved in decisions that his subordinates are being paid to make. So he stopped making them, and they tell me he plays a lot of golf in the time he saves," said Johnson.

Then I asked Johnson whether he tried to get MacGregor to make a decision and his response was:

"Only once. I had been on the job for only about a week when I ran into an operating problem I couldn't solve, so I phoned MacGregor. He answered the phone with that sleepy 'Hello' of his. I told him who I was and that I had a problem. His response was instantaneous: 'Good, that's what you're being paid to do, solve problems,' and then he hung up. I was dumbfounded. I didn't really know any of the people I was working with, so because I didn't think I had any other alternative, I called him back, got the same sleepy 'Hello,' and again identified myself. He replied sharply, 'I thought I told you that you were paid to solve problems. Do you think that I should do your job as well as my own?' When I insisted on seeing him about my problem, he answered, 'I don't know how you expect me to help you. You have a technical problem and I don't go into the refinery any more; I used to, but my shirts kept getting dirty from the visits and my wife doesn't like washing all the grime out of them, so I pretty much stick in my office. Ask one of the other men. They're all in touch with what goes on out there.'

"I didn't know which one to consult, so I insisted again on seeing him. He finally agreed—grudgingly—to see me right away, so I went over to his office and there he was in his characteristic looking-out-the-window posture. When I sat down, he started the dirty-shirt routine, but when he saw that I was determined to involve him in my problems, he sat down on the sofa in front of his coffee table and, pen in hand, prepared to write on a pad of paper. He asked me to state precisely what the problem was and he wrote down exactly what I said. Then he asked what the conditions for its solution were. I replied that I didn't know what he meant by that question. His response was 'If you don't know what conditions have to be satisfied for a solution to be reached, how do you know when you've solved the problem?' I told him I'd never thought of approaching a problem that way and he replied, 'Then you'd better start. I'll work through this one with you this time, but don't expect me to do your problem solving for you because that's your job, not mine.'

"I stumbled through the conditions that would have to be satisfied by the solution. Then he asked me what alternative approaches I could think of. I gave him the first one I could think of—let's call it X—and he wrote it down and asked me what would happen if I did X. I replied with my answer—let's call it A. Then he asked me how A compared with the conditions I had established for the solution of the problem. I replied that it did not meet them. MacGregor told me that I'd have to think of another. I came up with Y, which I said would yield result B, and this still fell short of the solution conditions. After more prodding from MacGregor, I came up with Z, which I said would have C as a result; although this clearly came a lot closer to the conditions I had established for the solution than any of the others I'd suggested, it still did not satisfy all of them. MacGregor then asked me if I could combine any of the approaches I'd suggested. I replied I could do X and Z and then saw that the resultant A plus C would indeed satisfy all the solution conditions I had set up previously. When I thanked MacGregor, he replied, 'What for? Get the hell out of my office; you could have done that bit of problem solving perfectly well without wasting my time. Next time you really can't solve a problem on your own, ask the Thursday man and tell me about it at the Thursday meeting.' "

I asked Johnson about Mr. MacGregor's reference to the Thursday man.

"He's the guy who runs the Thursday meeting when MacGregor is away from the plant. I'm the Thursday man now. My predecessor left here about two months ago."

"Where did he go? Did he quit the company?" I asked.

"God, no. He got a refinery of his own. That's what happens to a lot of Thursday men. After the kind of experience we get coping with everyone's problems and MacGregor's refusal to do what he perceives as his subordinates' work, we don't need an operating superior any more and we're ready for our own refineries. Incidentally, most of the people at our level here have adopted MacGregor's managerial method in dealing with the foremen who report to us, and we are reaping the same kinds of benefits that he does. The foremen are a lot more self-reliant, and we don't have to do their work for them."

I went back to see MacGregor. His secretary was still knitting. The garment she was working on was considerably more advanced than it was on my first visit. She motioned me into MacGregor's office with her head, again not dropping a stitch. MacGregor was in his traditional office posture, looking vacantly out of the window. He turned and asked, "Well, now do you believe that I don't make any decisions?"

I said, "No, that could have been just a fluke." He suggested I see another subordinate and asked me to pick another name from the list. I picked Peterson who, when phoned to see whether he was available, said that he had nothing to do. So I went to Peterson's office.

Peterson was in his late twenties. He asked me what I thought of MacGregor. I said I found him most unusual. Peterson replied, "Yes, he's a gas." Peterson's story paralleled Johnson's. MacGregor refused to make decisions related to the work of his subordinates. When Peterson got into a situation he could not deal with, he said he called one of the other supervisors, usually Johnson, and together they worked it out. At the Thursday meetings, he reported on the decision and gave credit to his helper. "If I don't," he added, "I probably wouldn't get help from that quarter again."

In reply to a query about the Thursday meetings, he said, "Well, we all sit around that big conference table in MacGregor's office. He sits at the head like a thinned-down Buddha, and we go around the table talking about the decisions we've made and, if we got help, who helped us. The other guys occasionally make comments, especially if the particular decision being discussed was like one they had had to make themselves at some point or if it had some direct effect on their own operations." MacGregor had said very little at these past few meetings, according to Peterson, but he did pass on any new developments that he heard about at the head office.

Head-Office Assessment of MacGregor

By the time I had finished with Johnson and Peterson, it was time for lunch. I decided I'd go downtown and stop in at the head office to try to find out their assessment of MacGregor and his operation. I visited the operations chief for the corporation. I had wanted to thank him for his willingness to go along with my study, anyway. When I told him I had met MacGregor, his immediate response was, "Isn't he a gas?" I muttered something about having heard that comment before and asked him about the efficiency of MacGregor's operation in comparison with that of other refineries in the corporation. His response was instantaneous, "Oh, MacGregor has by far the most efficient producing unit."

"Is that because he has the newest equipment?" I asked.

"No. As a matter of fact he has the oldest in the corporation. His was the first refinery we built."

"Does MacGregor have a lot of turnover among his subordinates?"

"A great deal," he replied.

Thinking I had found a chink in the MacGregor armor, I asked, "What happens to them; can't they take his system?"

"On the contrary," said the operations chief, "most of them go on to assignments as refinery managers. After all, under MacGregor's method of supervision, they are used to working on their own."

More Pointers on MacGregor's Style of Managing

"How do they run their own operations—like MacGregor's?" I asked.

"You guessed it. More and more of our managers are using his system."

I went back to the refinery with a few last questions for MacGregor. His secretary had made considerable progress on her knitting and her boss had resumed his position by the refinery window.

"I understand you were downtown. What did they tell you about this place?"

"You know damn well what they said—that you have the most efficient operation in the corporation."

"Yup, it's true," he replied, with no pretense at false modesty. "Periodically, I get chances to go to work for another major oil company, but I've gotten things so well organized here that I really don't want to take on a job like the one I faced when I came here five years ago. I guess I'll hang on here until something better comes up."

"Let me ask you a couple of questions about the Thursday meeting," I continued. "First of all, I understand that when you are away, the 'Thursday man' takes over. How do you choose the individual to fill this slot?"

"Oh, that's simple. I just pick the man who is most often referred to as the one my subordinates turn to for help in dealing with their problems. Then I try him out in this assignment while I'm off. It's good training and, if he proves he can handle it, I know I have someone to propose for any vacancies that may occur at the refinery manager level. The head-office people always contact me for candidates. As a matter of fact, the Thursday-man assignment is sought after. My subordinates compete with each other in helping anyone with a problem because they know they'll get credit for their help at the Thursday meeting. You know, another development has been that jobs on the staff of this refinery are highly prized by young people who want to get ahead in the corporation; when junior management positions open up here, there are always so many candidates that I often have a tough time making a choice."

"Sounds logical," I said. "Now let me focus a bit more on your role as refinery manager. You say you don't make decisions. Suppose a subordinate told you at a Thursday meeting about a decision he'd made and you were convinced that it was a mistake. What would yo do about it?"

"How much would the mistake cost me?"

"Oh, I don't know," I answered.

"Can't tell you, then. It would depend on how much it would cost."

"Say, $3,000," I suggested.

"That's easy; I'd let him make it," said MacGregor. I sensed I'd hit the upper limit before MacGregor either would have moved in himself or, more likely, would have suggested that the subordinates discuss it with the Thursday man and then report back to him on their joint decision.

"When was the last time you let a subordinate make a mistake of that magnitude?" I asked skeptically.

"About four weeks ago," said MacGregor.

"You let someone who works for you make such a serious mistake? Why did you do that?"

"Three reasons," said MacGregor. "First, I was only 99.44 percent sure it would be a mistake, and if it hadn't turned out to be one, I'd have felt pretty foolish. Second, I thought that making a mistake like this one would be such a tremendous learning experience for him that he'd never make another like that one again. I felt it would do him more good than signing him up for most of the management-development courses that are available. Third, this is a profit center. It was early in the budget year and I felt that we could afford it."

"What was the result?" I asked.

"It was a mistake—and I heard about it in short order from the controller downtown by phone." (I realized suddenly that during the whole time I had been in the office, neither MacGregor's phone nor his secretary's had rung.)

"The controller asked, 'MacGregor, how could you let a stupid mistake like that last one slip through?' "

"What did you say?"

"Well, I figured a good attack is best defense. I asked him which refinery in the corporation was the most efficient. He replied, 'You know yours is. That has nothing to do with it.' I told him that it had everything to do with it. I added that my people learn from their mistakes and that until the rest of the plants in the organization started operating at the same degree of efficiency as this one, I wasn't going to waste my time talking to clerks. Then I hung up."

"What happened?"

"Well, relations were a bit strained for a while, but they know I'm probably the best refinery manager in the business and I can get another job anytime, so it blew over pretty quickly," he said, not without a degree of self-satisfaction.

MacGregor's Control Systems

"Peterson told me you have quite a control system here. How does it work?" I asked.

"Very simply," said MacGregor. "On Wednesdays at 2:00 p.m. my subordinates and I get the printout from the computer, which shows the production men their output against quota and the maintenance superintendent his costs to date against the budget. If there is an unfavorable gap between the two, they call me about 3:00 p.m. and the conversation goes something like this: 'Mr. MacGregor, I know I have a problem and this is what I'm going to do about it.' If their solution will work, I tell them to go ahead. If not, I tell them so and then they go and work on it some more and then call back. If the new one will work, I tell them to go ahead with it. If not, I suggest they get in touch with one of the other men, work it out together, and then call me and tell me how they are going to deal with it. If that doesn't work, I refer them to the Thursday man. That way, I don't get involved in making operating decisions.

"I used to have a smaller refinery than this one, where I found myself frantically busy all the time—answering the phone constantly and continually doing my subordinates' problem solving for them. They were always more than willing to let me do their work because it was easier than doing it themselves and also because, if the solution did not work out, then I was to blame. Can't fault them for trying that. But when I came here, I resolved to get myself out of that kind of 'rat race' and set about designing this system. I worked out a computer-based production control system in conjunction with a set of quotas I negotiate each year with each of my operating people and a cost budget with the maintenance man. Then I arranged for Wednesday reports. Sometimes it takes a bit of time to renegotiate these quotas—and I've been known to use peer pressure to get them to a reasonable level—but these performance objectives really have to be accepted by the individual before they have any legitimacy or motivational value for him. I chose Wednesday because if a problem does develop, I still have time to act on my own if my subordinates can't come up with a solution. You see, our production week ends Saturday night. I don't want my head to fall in the basket because of their inability to make good decisions, so I minimized the risk this way.

"I can't even remember when I've had to get directly involved myself with their work. I do a lot of reading related to my work. That's why, when they call me with solutions, I can usually tell accurately whether or not their proposals are going to work out. That's my job as I see it—not doing subordinates' work but, rather, exercising supervision. A lot of managers feel that they have to keep proving to their people that they know more about their subordinates' jobs than the subordinates themselves by doing their work for them. I refuse to do that anymore."

"Is there anything else you do?" I asked.

"Well, I look after community relations. One more thing. I work on these." He stepped over to the engineer's file cabinet in the corner of his office. "In here are manning and equipment tables for this plant at five levels of production—at one-year, two-year, five-year, and ten-year intervals. If I get a phone call from the head office and they ask me what it would take to increase production by 20 percent, I ask over what period; if they say, for example, five years, I just read off the equipment and the personnel that would be needed. That's what I see as being an upper-level manager's job. As I recall, Peter Drucker once said that managers get paid for the futurity and irreversibility of the decisions they make. Well, these sorts of decisions are way in the future and are terribly difficult and expensive to reverse once they are embarked on. Too many managers say they have no time to plan; yet that's what they are being paid to do, not to do their subordinates' work. Not me; I plan, listen to Wednesday reports and Thursday decisions, and play golf."

"Do your subordinates help you make these planning decisions?" I asked.

"No," said MacGregor. "They gather some of the information and I show them how I go about making up the plans. They all know how to do it after they've been here a couple of years. The actual decisions, though, are made by me. If they are wrong, I have to take the blame. And if they are right," he said with a smile, "I take the credit. Now, I have a most important golf game scheduled. If you have any further questions, just come in any time except Thursday between 10:00 a.m. and noon. I don't have much to do except to talk to visitors."

As I drove back home, I started to think about the MacGregor approach to management. Did MacGregor use job enrichment? Yes, his men were motivated by their jobs themselves. Did MacGregor train his subordinates? Evidently, because they seem to be constantly in line for promotion. And there was certainly no doubt about the efficiency of his operation. No question about it: MacGregor was a well-organized manager who still had enough time to work on his golf game.

MacGregor Epilogue

It is clear that MacGregor had several things going for him that helped make his system effective. Not the least of these was that he had very precise measures of the output of each of his subordinates—barrels or product of performance against budget. It is also true that he was in charge of a profit center and that his own performance was appraised over a time span sufficiently long for him to offset short-term diminished performance with long-term results. Further, MacGregor's responsibilities were confined to production; he did not have to contend with marketing problems. His job was merely to deliver a line of products in the quantities called for at minimum cost, by means of production processes that had been well established and understood by those in charge of them. Certainly all these factors helped MacGregor run his operation the way he did, and there is no doubt that as his reputation became established, his superiors gave him a freer hand. But to explain MacGregor in terms of a fit between his leadership style and the nature of his responsibilities is to deny what he tells us about how the really effective manager performs his functions.

MacGregor's overriding concern was with results—the results his subordinates achieved through methods they developed either by themselves or by working with their peers. He simply refused to do their work for them, even at the risk of incurring short-run costs. By refusing, he enabled them to grow in terms of their ability to make decisions even under conditions of uncertainty. MacGregor's contact with his subordinates centered on the negotiation of performance standards and the receipt of progress reports on the results they were achieving. When their performance fell short of these standards, he saw his role as one of reminding them that they had a problem and that he was interested in hearing how they were going to deal with it. If they could not solve it themselves (and he was confident that he was technically able to assess the likelihood that their solution would be successful), he referred them to one of their peers. He would not permit them to become dependent on him as the ultimate problem solver, ever ready to prove his technical proficiency and perfectly willing to be Big Daddy to subordinates in distress. For MacGregor, each problem encountered by his subordinates represented a self-teaching opportunity. He recognized that he was ultimately responsible for finding the right answer to the problem, but not for formulating its solution, and that for him to become involved in his subordinates' responsibilities was to assume part of the burden that was appropriately their own. Perhaps even more importantly, doing so would be to deny them the chance to develop their own problem-solving abilities. This refusal to involve himself in their activities afforded him the opportunity to fulfill the planning obligations inherent in higher-level management assignments.

Essential to MacGregor's system of management was a team of subordinates highly committed to their job objectives. This commitment was achieved by negotiation of the specific results each was to accomplish, and these negotiations continued until both sides were satisfied that they were realistic and attainable. When a subordinate suggested unrealistic objectives, on either the low or the high side, they were modified through open discussion with both sides willing to adjust previously held positions. In all cases MacGregor left specifics on how agreed-upon results were to be achieved to the subordinates themselves. By insisting that he be informed on how decisions were actually made, including who helped in the process, MacGregor not only ensured that his subordinates helped each other, but also received the information that he needed to make valid judgments on how well each of them was developing in his job.

Because of the record his subordinates achieved in receiving promotions to the position of refinery manager, MacGregor had no trouble attracting highly capable candidates for managerial jobs in his refinery. Once on his staff, managers recognized that the way to become a Thursday man was through a combination of high performance and an ability to work with peers in a way that enabled them to solve their own problems and reach their own objectives.

Uniqueness of MacGregor

MacGregor was unique among the managers I interviewed in the course of my study. Presumably his approach was a distinct possibility for each of the nine refinery managers I talked to, and certainly with adaptions it could have been used by many of the 100 executives I interviewed. But it wasn't. He had taken management by objectives to its logical limits by concentrating his efforts on formulating and negotiating objectives and had divorced himself from direct involvement in solving problems his subordinates came upon in carrying out their responsibilities.

MacGregor's frequency of regularly scheduled meetings with his subordinates was typical of the managers interviewed in the study: 10 percent met less frequently and about 5 percent more often. But his focus on discussion of completed decisions was unique. Slightly less than three-quarters of the executives with whom I talked saw the purpose of their meetings as a combination of information communication and problem solving; the balance were split evenly between a primary focus on communication of information and a primary emphasis on problem solving. Interestingly, the majority of those who emphasized problem solving were refinery executives.

When describing the degree of reliance they placed on the contributions made by subordinates in the determination of final decisions, half of the managers felt that it was considerable, a quarter that it was heavy, and the balance that it was either not too significant or that it varied with the individuals involved. Only MacGregor left the actual decision making (except in rare circumstances) to the subordinates themselves.

All the managers, except MacGregor, either stated explicitly or made it clear during the course of the interviews that all important decisions arrived at in these meetings were made by themselves. They received suggestions, considered their sources, and either compared the proffered solutions with solutions they had developed on their own, or considered them carefully before reaching a final solution. In using this approach to group decision making, the managers were obviously manifesting their deeply held convictions that one of the key responsibilities of an upper-level executive is to act as chief decision maker for those who report to him. They believed that, after all, the superior is ultimately responsible for the quality of the decisions made in his organization and that the only way to carry out this task is to become directly involved in the decision-making process itself.

Most of the managers I have encountered—both organizational superiors and outside managers involved in the studies I've conducted or the consulting assignments I've carried out—pride themselves on the extent to which they invite their subordinates to participate in organizational decision making; but their perceptions of this process and its organizational impact often differ sharply from those of the subordinates involved. For many of the latter, the participative management routine is just that—a routine acted out by the boss because it evidences his espousal of a technique that is supposed to increase the likelihood that subordinates will accept and commit themselves to decisions; he may even believe the decisions were jointly determined. However, most participative management is, in fact, a fiction. Under these conditions, participative management is seen by lower-level participants, as, at worst, a manipulative device and at best an opportunity for them to avoid decision-making responsibility and assure that if a wrong solution is reached, the boss himself was a party to the decision.

MacGregor avoided this trap by refusing to give managers reporting to him the opportunity to second-guess the solution he would be most likely to choose. Although he allowed himself some margin in case emergency action on his part should become inevitable, he made it clear that he wanted to hear about problems only after they had been solved and about decisions only after they had been made.

Perspective on MacGregor's Use of Time

It is interesting to compare MacGregor's use of time, which perhaps better than any other index shows his priorities, with the findings reported by management researchers who have conducted detailed quantitative studies of the way managers perform their jobs. In two articles—"A New Look at the Chief Executive's Job," *Organizational Dynamics* (Winter 1973, pp. 20-30) and "The Manager's Job: Folklore and Fact," *Harvard Business Review* (July-August 1975, pp. 49-61)—Henry Mintzberg cites the work of Rosemary Steward, Leonard Sayles, Robert Guest, and others on the work characteristics of managers and then develops ten roles of the chief executive, which he divides into three groupings: interpersonal, informational, and decisional. Under the interpersonal classification, Mintzberg includes such roles as figurehead, leader, and liaison; under informational, monitor, disseminator, and spokesman; and under decisional, entrepreneur (seeking to improve his unit and adapt it to changing conditions in the environment), disturbance handler, resource allocator, and negotiator.

The job of refinery manager falls between that of chief executive (responsibility for all aspects of the operation and profit accountability) and that of production manager (only indirect concern for the integration of such functions as finance, accounting, marketing, and so on). Mintzberg points out that production managers give greatest attention to decisional roles, especially those of disturbance handler and negotiator. MacGregor, by contrast, minimized his role as disturbance handler but did put a lot of time, energy, and effort into negotiating objectives with his subordinates rather than laying them on his people and then selling them on the reasonableness of his decisions. He also worked constantly to improve his unit, to adapt it to changing environmental conditions, and to allocate present and potential organizational resources for optimal present and future effectiveness. In his interpersonal role MacGregor was readily available for figurehead and liaison activities, and his program for subordinate self-development attracted enough attention within the corporation to ensure a supply of highly motivated subordinates.

In his informational role, MacGregor monitored the output of the management information system he had devised, but he did so after the same information had been reviewed by his subordinates. The dissemination function was partly achieved by the management information system and partly through the joint review of managerial decisions conducted at the Thursday morning meetings. As spokesman for his unit, he was easily accessible to individuals inside and outside the corporation.

What sets MacGregor apart from other managers is that he had consciously thought out his role as an upper-level administrator. He did not blindly adopt the methods of his predecessor; neither did he merely adapt the *modus operandi* he had previously found reasonably successful to the greater demands of running a larger unit. Rather, MacGregor reflected on what the key responsibilities of the executive in charge of a large operating facility really are and concluded that they involve being well informed on changes occurring in the environment that might have an impact on his operation and determining how best to adjust operations to benefit from these changes. At the same time, MacGregor recognized that profitable operations must be carried out in the here-and-now and that a supply of qualified subordinates must be developed for the future.

He concluded that his time was the scarce commodity, and he threw himself into the design and implementation of a managerial system that had as its hallmarks self-development for his subordinates, efficient operation for his employer, and time for himself to consider actively the impact of future developments on his unit. His wise investment of that scarce commodity, his own time, in designing an effective management system paid an extra dividend—surplus time for recreational pursuits.